DOGS and Their PEOPLE

DOGS and Their PEOPLE

PHOTOS AND STORIES OF LIFE WITH A FOUR-LEGGED LOVE

A BarkBook by BarkPost®

Morgane Chang and Stacie Grissom
Illustrations by Dave Coverly

Bark & Co. | BarkBox | BarkShop | BarkPost

G. P. PUTNAM'S SONS
NEW YORK

To dogs: Thanks for being our best buds for the past 31,000 years.

DOGS
and Their
PEOPLE

FAMILY

(fam-i-lee) n.

1. You love them and they love you.

2. You trust them and they trust you.

3. You take care of them and they take care of you.

4. You know each other by heart...and by fart.

These pages celebrate the couch-snuggling, belly-scratching, snout-kissing humans who share their lives with dogs.

We, like you, are dog people.

We dedicate these stories to the millions of us out there who share a special connection to these furry dumplings and know how much richer life is with a dog by our side.

Here are just a few of the infinite reasons that demonstrate the lengths you would go out of a kooky, insatiable love for your dog.

CRICKET BEAN, ONE OF THE EARLIEST
BARK & CO. PUPLOYEES

YOU STARTED A COMPANY WITH THE SOLE MISSION TO MAKE DOGS HAPPY.

I'm obsessed with my dog, a Great Dane named Hugo. I was looking for ways to make Hugo happy with a new toy or treat that was perfect for him but found it very challenging.

I shared that with Henrik, and we thought of the monthly box idea with products that are perfect for your dog. Selling to a million people didn't really matter as long as my dog loved it. We're a company that exists to make dogs and their people happy. We have toys and treats for dogs, entertainment for dogs and their people, experiences for dogs and their people, and so much more coming in the future. I'm telling you, in the next five years I will fly on a commercial flight with my Great Dane in the cabin, and we'll be responsible for that.

Matt Meeker & Hugo
CO-FOUNDER OF BARK & CO.

In the first days of Bark & Co., my wife and I fostered dogs constantly. Fostering opened my eyes to so many issues in the dog world that I never noticed before.

I wanted to find a way to scale my donation to dogs in need and realized that in order to help millions of dogs, I needed to build a company where that mission was a part of the DNA. Today and always, helping dogs in need is a core value of the Bark ethos.

When my wife became pregnant, we decided to find one dog that could become our son's best friend. We met our dog, Molly, through a rescue organization that brought her up from the streets of Mobile, Alabama. Molly is now a constant inspiration that forces me to think of new experiences I can have with her that make her happy. I feel that part of the reason we have been so successful in launching new products and services is that it's all anchored in our love for our own dogs.

Henrik Werdelin & Molly
CO-FOUNDER OF BARK & CO.

When I was growing up, we didn't have big pet stores in upstate New York. Our town had a local dog bakery and a very small pet boutique. I grew accustomed to exploring small and local brands and being able to treat my dogs, Cooper and Roxy, to something more unique and special.

I later realized that everyone hadn't had the same experience as my own. That became, and still is, a huge part of Bark—discovering amazing experiences out there and personalizing it all for your dog.

I had explored several career paths since college, from engineering to finance to operations. When I started to think about what I really cared about and what made me happy every day, the only things that stood out were my dogs. I never thought I'd actually have the opportunity to mix my career focus and my passion, and when I met Henrik and Matt, I thought I was dreaming.

Carly Strife, Roxy & Cooper
CO-FOUNDER OF BARK & CO.

TIMELINE OF BARK & CO.

DECEMBER
2011

Bark & Co. ships its first BarkBox from Chinatown, NYC. Founders Matt, Carly, and Henrik pay friends in pizza to help pack boxes of toys and treats to send to lucky pups across the country. Henrik, originally from Denmark, writes "Happy Hollidays" with two *l*'s in many of them accidentally.

AUGUST
2011

The rise of celebridogs like Boo, Tuna, and the Doge meme hit mainstream.

OCTOBER
2012

BarkPost.com launches to bring dog stories, videos, and memes to the world.

DECEMBER
2012

@BarkBox publishes its first Instagram post, falling into the dazzling rabbit hole of Internet pup parents.

NOVEMBER
2012

Bark designs, develops, and ships the first BarkMade toy: a bouquet of plush, squeaky flowers.

JUNE
2013

BarkPost hosts a Willy Wonka–style "Golden Bone" video contest and flies Watson the Schnauzer out to Bark HQ for the ultimate NYC dog tour.

JULY
2013

BarkPost hosts a "Pup-up Adoption Shop" in Soho and every single dog went to a furever home that day.

OCTOBER
2014

BarkShop.com opens its virtual doors as Bark & Co.'s first retail e-commerce site.

JANUARY
2014

Bark & Co. moves to a larger office designed with the dogs in mind first, humans second. Cartoonist Dave Coverly covers the office in custom illustrations. Office dog Brownie christens the new space with a legendary pee straight into a trash can.

MARCH
2015

Bark & Co. flies the whole company, now fifty-five employees, to Disney World.

OCTOBER
2016

You've got it in your paws right now: BarkBook is pup-lished!

(bark) n.

1. A dog's way of saying "I don't see anything, but there could still be something there, and everyone needs to know about it."
   See also: 2am Activitie

JULY
2015

BarkLive throws its second annual BarkFest, where ten thousand dog lovers flock to the Brooklyn waterfront for the biggest dog event in NYC.

YOU SET UP AN INSTAGRAM ACCOUNT FOR YOUR DOG BECAUSE HIS SMILE NEEDED TO BE SHARED WITH THE WORLD.

Dexter the miniature Dachshund first became dog-famous on Vine with over 125,000 loyal fans. BuzzFeed named him "The Happiest Dog in the World" because of his big Dumbo ears, his winning smile, and the fact that his tail never stops wagging! I think he would like to be known as "Dexter the Happy Dachshund" someday. He acts very nervous and yet so excited at the same time—you can't help but fall in love with his big brown eyes. He has melted many hearts all over the world and there are still more to come!

Karen & Dexter
BUENA PARK, CALIFORNIA
 DEXTYTHEDACHSHUND

YOU TALKED ABOUT YOUR DOG LIKE SHE WAS YOURS BEFORE YOU HAD EVEN MET HER.

I was not planning on adopting another dog until I saw Ivy. Her kennel card photo was heartbreaking. She was a nine-month-old, fourteen-pound stray. She had a skin infection, missing fur, and a wound around her neck, likely from an embedded collar. Her kill date was in six days. I posted her photo to social media begging someone to adopt her, but in my heart, I already knew she would end up with me. In fact, I had already named her.

When I finally got to meet Ivy, she lay down on my feet and I knew she was coming home with me. That first day, she followed me around as if we had known each other forever; it was as if she knew we belonged together. I signed the adoption papers that very day. I visited her as much as I could until she got spayed, and finally, I brought her home. My dog Sookie and Ivy have been best friends ever since!

Jannina, Sookie & Ivy
ROCKPORT, MASSACHUSETTS
:camera: SOOKIEANDIVY

A SIMPLE GUIDE TO ADOPTING A DOG

✳ If you feel that you're ready to adopt from a rescue group, consult your local shelters, foster groups, and animal care and control organizations by visiting their website or giving them a call. The Shelter Pet Project, American Society for the Prevention of Cruelty to Animals (ASPCA), and Petfinder websites are also useful resources.

✳ Visit the shelter, meet the dogs, or sign up for the organization's e-mails.

✳ When you find a dog you'd like to adopt, you will likely be asked to fill out an application, and often you can add your name to a waiting list. Reputable shelters and rescue groups will conduct a detailed analysis of a dog's behavior to better ensure that you and your new pup are a good fit, and they may do a home check.

✳ *Foster:* If you're not quite ready to adopt, fostering a dog is a fantastic option. You'll get a better sense of what your next step is, you'll help a dog prepare for their furever home, and you'll free up a spot at the local shelter for another pup in need.

✳ *Remember:* It's important to be clear and honest throughout the process so that you can be matched with the dog that is best suited for your lifestyle and personality.

YOU ASSEMBLED A SQUAD OF NAKED DOGS AND MADE THEM YOUR FAMILY.

My passion for hairless breeds brought me to the Bald Is Beautiful community, and it wasn't long before I fostered Nathan. Bald Is Beautiful Hairless and Small Breed Rescue, Inc. is a national nonprofit organization that specializes in the rescue and placement of abused, unwanted, and abandoned dogs. It concentrates on hairless and small-breed dogs but never discriminates on the basis of health, age, or breed.

Although Nathan and I bonded right away, he was confused and insecure and showed major fear aggression toward other humans and dogs. I was not planning to adopt another dog, but when his pending adoption fell through, Nathan and I made a deal. He would stay with me and reign as the primary ambassador for Bald Is Beautiful.

Nathan is thriving and has transitioned into a much more social, happy-go-lucky, loving, and confident dog. He proves that damaged dogs can be rehabilitated (and even become famous!) if they're shown patience, love, and attention. Through the attention Nathan has garnered, his rescue has benefited. Inquiries about and interest in the breed have increased awareness, and comments have been more positive than ever.

Thanks to Bald Is Beautiful, our naked squad is bigger than just my six dogs. The rescue throws biannual "nekkid parties" to celebrate the rescue's ongoing successes. In the fall of 2015, Bald Is Beautiful celebrated five years with its High Five Party in Myrtle Beach, South Carolina. Over 75 people—including volunteers, adopters, and friends, and even more dogs—enjoyed a weekend of camaraderie that included workshops on grooming and photography, as well as an auction, a fashion show, and a Halloween costume contest.

Tina, Nathan, Demi, Gilligan, Kramer & Chip
SEAFORD, VIRGINIA DANCINGNATHAN

DEMI

Adopted in 2009, Demi is a perfect little princess who typically stays in the background while the boys get all the attention. Even so, she's got them all beat on beauty, grace, and manners. She's considered a "Hairy Hairless" Chinese Crested.

NATHAN

Not only does Nathan have a unique appearance, he also smiles, dances, and happens to have the best sidekicks! Nathan's mission is to use all these special blessings to be an ambassador for Bald Is Beautiful by spreading awareness, love, and joy.

"HOT MESS" GILLIGAN

Gilligan is small and bossy. He doesn't hesitate to tattle when someone (ahem, Nathan) misbehaves. Gilligan was rescued with quite a few others from a hoarding situation. His mission in life is to be held by *anyone*—he's not picky. His deadpan manner, captured in photos, is a cover. He's actually a big baby who is spoiled rotten and throws tantrums. He's a real-life cartoon character.

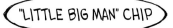

"LITTLE BIG MAN" CHIP

Chip was here before all the nekkid critters moved in. He's a ten-pound Yorkshire Terrier with a huge attitude. He'll be thirteen years old in March and is now blind, arthritic, and allergic to everything. As long as he stays grumpy, I know he's okay.

KRAMER

Kramer was my very first Chinese Crested "Prince Charming." Kramer, who will soon turn ten years old, is responsible for starting my obsession with the breed. He blasts into a room just like Kramer on *Seinfeld*. I feel comfortable telling him he's in charge when I go anywhere.

YOU ACCEPT THAT PUTTING IN EARPLUGS IN PREPARATION FOR A 7.0 PUG-SNORE EARTHQUAKE IS JUST PART OF YOUR NIGHTLY ROUTINE.

I know I love Homer dearly because I put up with his snoring habit—and man, can a Pug really snore! I have to use earplugs every night.

Mei & Homer
PERTH, AUSTRALIA
HOMERPUGALICIOUS

YOU SPEND HOURS STICKING YOUR DOG INTO EVERY COSTUME FOR THAT PERFECT PICTURE.

One of Maymo's favorite pastimes is destroying stuffed animals. I learned this firsthand when he tore off the face of an antique panda bear that had been in my family for generations. After the initial shock of finding the maimed panda wore off, I decided I would do what any responsible dog parent would—I used the panda as a costume for Maymo, filmed a video of the affair, and posted it on YouTube. The video was a success and Maymo himself loved the whole process; he got copious treats for sitting still in the costume and after filming was allowed to destroy the faceless stuffed animal. This is how Maymo's career as a dog in disguise started.

Jeremy & Maymo
MERRIMACK VALLEY, MASSACHUSETTS 📷 MAYMOTHEDOG

TIPS FOR GETTING THE PERFECT INSTAGRAM SHOT OF YOUR PUP

Have some fun props ready. Suggestions include a pair of sunglasses, a shiny wig, or a massive mermaid tail.

Set the stage. Is your dog an astronaut? Make sure to set up a background with glow-in-the-dark stars. Is your dog Queen Elizabeth? Build a midsized replica of Buckingham Palace.

Use every trick in your book to catch your dog's best facial expression. Make silly voices, wave a treat or a toy above the lens of your camera, and give your pup a pep talk ("You WILL be a celebridog, You CAN reach ten thousand followers, I can SMELL IT!").

Get a friend to assist. Have someone hold a tasty spoonful of peanut butter while you take an A+ adorbs picture. After all, your dog is a budding superstar—they should get used to having a staff.

Remember: If you don't get it right on the first shot, you can always take forty-five more.

YOU TAUGHT YOUR DEAF DOG SIGN LANGUAGE.

After rescuing my dog Miller, we discovered that he was deaf. We bought a handbook of American Sign Language and embarked on training both ourselves and Miller. We started with "good job," which we signed with a thumbs-up. Once he mastered the meaning of that, we went on to "sit." The training continued and he has now mastered over thirty signs! While he knows the typical commands, we've also taught him several unique signs. Some are to provide direction, including crossing straight through an intersection when we are on a run or signaling for him to go to his bed. Others are designed to ask him questions to find out if he is hungry or thirsty or needs to go outside. Then there are the ones we

designed to make him feel safe. We developed four different signs that collectively mean: "Hello, your dad is still here and I'll be back soon. I love you."

Miller adores people, and we take him to different places so that he can become more confident in new surroundings. Ultimately, we want to be a good ambassador for deaf dogs. Deaf dogs are smart, happy, loving, and very trainable with the right form of communication. Miller has taught us so much more than I ever imagined. The girls in our vet's reception area say he "listens" better than many of the hearing dogs they see! I couldn't agree more.

Libby & Miller
DAVENPORT, FLORIDA

TEACH YOUR DOG SIGN LANGUAGE

I love you

good job

sit

no

YOU BECAME A PERSONAL TRAINER FOR YOUR DOG.

Although I'm personally health conscious, I admit that I allowed my dog Charlie to become overweight. Because of the Dachshund's unique shape, added weight puts extra stress on their backs that can lead to serious injury, including paralysis. I realized it was time to take control of my dog's caloric intake, so I factored in Charlie's weight and activity level, made a daily meal plan, and meticulously weighed each of Charlie's meals to make sure he was consuming the right amount of food. After many weeks, Charlie's weight was down almost twenty-five percent, and he can now play and run around at the dog park!

Miguel & Charlie
WHITE PLAINS, NEW YORK
CHARLIE.AND.MAGGIE

YOU KEEP FLANNEL SHEETS ON THE BED YEAR-ROUND TO KEEP YOUR DOG AS SNUGGLY AS POSSIBLE.

It all started a few years ago when we decided to take our bed off the frame to lower it. Why? So the puppy, Scruffy, could jump up on the bed without straining himself. Easy access, you know, for the baby. He likes to be tucked into the middle of the bed and have his right hind foot massaged as he falls asleep.

We noticed that Scruffy also preferred to lie on the soft flannel blankets and sheets of our bed rather than the percale sheets. The simple solution: use flannel sheets on the bed year-round, and keep a fluffy fur blanket at the foot of the bed for good measure. Options. A dog likes options.

Michele & Scruffy
BELLEVUE, WASHINGTON 📷 SCRUFFY_IN_SEATTLE

YOU PASS ON YOUR DREAM APARTMENT BECAUSE IT IS TOO FAR FROM YOUR DOG'S FAVORITE PARK.

After an exhaustive two-month search, my boyfriend, Nelson, and I found the perfect little New York apartment. It was equipped with brand-new appliances, ample storage space, a sunny roof deck, and a coveted washer and dryer, and it was in our price range! However, with barely any deliberation at all, we decided to pass. It was simply too far from Oona's favorite place: Prospect Park. Who could disappoint that face? Amenities are overrated anyway...

Ally & Oona
BROOKLYN, NEW YORK ⊙ OONAISAGODDESS

YOU MAKE SURE YOUR DOG GETS SUFFICIENT KISSES EACH DAY.

I had wanted a Pug for as long as I could remember. I sent my now-husband photos and videos of Pugs daily, and it was only when I threatened to get pregnant that he surprised me with Charlie. It was love and loaf at first sight.

One day I counted the number of times I kissed Charlie. I stopped at 137. He finally kissed back.

Meredith & Charlie
SOMERVILLE, MASSACHUSETTS 📷 THISPUGSLIFE

Way back when Remix was a wee pup, my boyfriend and I were completely obsessed with him. His trot reminded us of sound effects we would hear in cartoons and we thought it would be really cool if he had his own theme song, too. We made something up on the spot to the tune of a few kids' songs, and that's how our secret song came about. To this day, when we sing the song, we always get so many tail wags from our little man!

YOU HAVE A SECRET SONG AND CHOREOGRAPHED DANCE ABOUT YOUR DOG THAT YOU PERFORM AROUND THE HOUSE.

Jennifer & Remix
TORONTO, ONTARIO
REMIXTHEDOG

THE HAWTEST DOG TRENDS

THE ELECTRIC SCOOT

COTTON-EYE DOGE

WATCH ME WOOF, WATCH ME PEE-PEE

DOGUE

THE PAW-CARENA

THE STINKY LEG

THE GRAPEWHINE

YOU CARE JUST AS MUCH ABOUT YOUR DOG'S VIEW AS YOUR OWN WHEN YOU GO CAMPING.

We took Penelope camping over the summer for two months—partly for our enjoyment, but mostly because we know how much she enjoys exploring the outdoors. For our entire trip, we let her sleep in our rooftop tent (quite literally a tent that is secured to the roof of our car) and carried our forty pounds of pup up and down the ten-step ladder, even when she had the occasional midnight potty break. She doubled as a heater and snuggle buddy, so we were happy to have her with us. When we weren't in the tent, Penelope's pops held her up so she could take in the beautiful view.

Melanny & Penelope
LAWRENCEVILLE, GEORGIA ⬛ 8LITTLEPAWS

ELEVEN TIPS ON HOW TO "RUFF IT" WITH YOUR DOG

1. Always have a collapsible water bowl and enough water for you and your pooch on hand.

2. Make sure the insect repellent you purchase is dog-friendly just in case your pup wanders toward you midspritz.

3. Check and make sure wherever you're going is dog-friendly! Hint: If it is bear-friendly...Big. Red. Flag.

4. Go glamping instead! It's like camping but so much more like not camping.

5. Avoid areas with tall grass, and be on the lookout for ticks! If your dog has a thick coat or floppy ears, make sure to do an extra thorough check in their fur and inside their ears.

6. Bring plenty of dog food for your pooch. He can totally eat off your barbecue plate if you want, but those are farts you're bringing upon yourself.

7. If you choose to go kayaking while camping, have a doggie life vest for your furry friend. Preferably a fashionable one. Just because you're in the wild doesn't mean you can skimp out on aesthetics.

8. Bring a cooling mat so your dog isn't as much of a hot, sweaty mess as you are.

9. Acquire a sturdy tent so as to prevent your dog from scratching through it. You never know when your dog is going to want to go exploring!

10. If it gets cold at night wherever you're camping, make sure to bring plenty of (fashionable) sweaters for your pup!

11. Make sure your dog is on a leash if you're staying in a campground. You never know how your camp neighbors will respond to a dog. Also, if your camp neighbors respond poorly to a dog, you should find a new spot.

HOW TO MAKE A SIMPLE BANDANA FOR YOUR DOG

There are many practical reasons for a dog to wear a bandana. Bandanas are fantastic drool bibs for slobber monsters, they help keep tabs at the dog park, and wet bandanas can be portable little air conditioners on a hot summer hike. But mostly...They just look really adorable.

SUPPLIES:

- Fabric
- Needle and thread or a sewing machine
- Iron

STEP 1: First, cut a square of fabric large enough to fit around your dog's noggin. When you fold the square in half diagonally, you should have an extra 1-2 inches of fabric to make sure the bandana comfortably fits around your pup's neck.

STEP 2: Fold the fabric in half with the pattern on the inside and iron it in place to make crisp lines before you sew. Stitch along the open sides of the bandana, leaving a two-inch gap on one of the sides. Flip the bandana right-side out, iron it in place, and stitch up the open hole you used to flip the bandana.

STEP 3: Hold the bandana up around your pup's neck to measure the proper width and stitch everything in place!

STEP 4: Admire your work on the cutest model you know. For advanced dog people, stage a photoshoot in the new bandana and post photos to your dog's social media accounts.

YOU ALMOST ALWAYS INVOLVE YOUR DOG IN YOUR DIY PROJECTS.

Ever since I was a little kid, I have always tried to incorporate my family dogs into my art projects. If my teacher Mrs. Decker assigned the class to make a construction paper collage, mine was the scene of my backyard with my black Lab, Daisy. Once Mrs. Decker told us to draw a still-life of a jug, and my artwork had the jug in the foreground and my dog through the window in the background. On another occasion, the class made life-sized holiday elves to display in the hallway. My elf had the shape of an eight-year-old human body and the face of a Labrador. Now that I have a dog of my own, not much has changed!

Stacie & Pimm
NEW YORK, NEW YORK ◉ PIMMPUP

MODERN RUV

(mod·ern ruv) n.

When you sniff butts at the dog park, but
it probably doesn't mean anything serious.

YOU ARE THE JEALOUS GIRLFRIEND IN YOUR RELATIONSHIP WITH YOUR DOG.

My dog, Benji, is my world. You could say we're in an exclusive relationship of sorts: the kind of relationship where I'm the needy girlfriend trying to get his attention while he just ignores me.

I'm not ashamed to admit that I get insanely jealous when he cuddles with my roommates or my friends. I also get offended on his behalf when people don't immediately exclaim, "He's so adorable" the instant they see him.

Tasmai & Sir Benjamin Barkington
BROOKLYN, NEW YORK 📷 THEDOGINABAG

"YOU'RE THE ONLY ONE WHO'S ALLOWED TO DO A DUTCH OVEN IN MY BED. THAT SHOULD TELL YOU HOW MUCH I LOVE YOU. NOW CAN WE TAKE A SELFIE WHERE YOU LOOK LIKE YOU MEAN IT?"

SPARKLING, TAP, OR TOILET?

TOILET (`toilit) n.
A butt-flavored water fountain. They are a delight.

HE EVEN PIDDLED ON THEM BEFORE HE GAVE THEM TO ME !

SO ROMANTIC !!

YOU WILL NEVER SETTLE FOR SOMEONE WHO DOESN'T TREAT YOUR DOG LIKE THE KING THAT HE IS.

Being able to live and work in New York City was always the setting for my when-I-grow-up fairy tale, but my bachelorette lifestyle looks a little different than the one I originally imagined.

When I adopted eight-year-old Benny, I was determined to give this incredibly spunky and amazingly sweet senior pup the best life possible. This included several knee surgeries to repair damage done by years of prior neglect and meant that my dog would be on restricted activity for the rest of his life. Years later, eleven-year-old Benny is mistaken for a puppy daily with his nonstop energy.

As a result, my bachelorette pad has the look of either a toddler's playroom or the home of a vertically challenged senior citizen. There's a mini stuffed staircase for Benny to get on the bed since he's not allowed to jump up or down. There are blankets all over the floor as makeshift carpeting so he won't slip. My studio apartment that lacks space for a dining table contains three dog beds.

Benny not only rules my apartment but also my personal life. After six months, one guy broke up with me because he said I was too obsessed with my dog. More, Benny once peed directly on the flip-flopped foot of what was a first (and ultimately only) date. And those after-work happy hours? With a guy as cute as Benny waiting for me at home, those generally consist of drinking boxed wine with my pup on my futon while watching Hulu.

If I didn't have Benny, it would be much easier to date. I certainly would have kissed a lot more frogs and maybe even met a prince, but I wouldn't have my little king. And without him, it simply wouldn't be a fairy tale.

Jenny & Benny
BROOKLYN, NEW YORK ⊙ ILUVLIZLEMON

YOU ENDURE INTENSE ALLERGIES TO KEEP THE ROMANCE ALIVE BETWEEN YOU AND YOUR DOG.

Waffles was initially not a fan of my husband, Jason, which my dog demonstrated by spilling an entire glass of red wine in his lap the first time he came over. Once football season started, though, it was a whole different story. Waffles discovered that Jason liked to lounge on the couch just like he did. In the process of their blooming romance, however, Jason developed a severe allergy to Waffles. His eyes were red all the time, he was constantly sneezing, and he was totally miserable. Poor Jason lived with this for weeks without telling me that Waffles was likely the culprit because he didn't want to upset me.

Today, he has the right allergy meds, but he has given up wearing contacts so that I can keep my best friend. Waffles is his best friend now, too.

Amanda & Waffles
CHICAGO, ILLINOIS
WAFFLESGRIFFON

Allergies, Shmallergies, am I right?

YOU HAVE ONLY GOT ROOM IN YOUR BED FOR ONE SPECIAL DUDE.

Fitzgerald and I have our nightly routine: we go outside for one last potty break for Fitz, I take one last potty break for myself while Fitz stares at me, and then we hop into bed and sleep peacefully side by side. So when another man came around and took Fitz's spot in bed, it was clear his canine heart was broken. Eventually, the thought of my baby Fitz lying sadly on the floor below became too much for me. I kicked Fitz's new nemesis to the couch so my #1 guy could be by my side. Needless to say, this is why I'm still single.

Lauren & Fitz
COLUMBUS, OHIO  HISSYFITZ

TOP 5

THINGS YOU LEARN WHEN YOU DATE A DOG LOVER

#5

You're going to be third-wheeling your S.O. and their dog about 94.7 percent of the time.

#4

They have a "Happens" attitude, so you know they'll always be your rock when you need one.

#3

They've got the goofiest, silliest, funniest sense of humor because, umm, dog farts are hilarious!

#2

They're loyal like whoa!

#1

Their love for you = their love for their dog, and you happily support it.

YOU CHOOSE RUVRIFE OVER YOUR LOVE LIFE.

As we lounged in the sun, my boyfriend asked me why I turned down so many social events. I answered, "Meg." He then asked me who is more important, him or my dog? I looked over to see Meg stealing his water bottle from his bag and racing toward the ocean with it in her mouth. He chased after her, shouting, and all I could do was laugh. When Meg returned soaked from her swim, she jumped on me. It was as if she knew the question I had just been asked. Although I deliberated, I ultimately chose Meg, and my boyfriend and I broke up. Who needs a boyfriend when you have a dog's unfaltering loyalty and unbeatable cuddles?

Charnia & Megatron
LANCASTER, UNITED KINGDOM BIGFATBROWNDOG

YOU LET YOUR DOG PICK YOUR BOYFRIENDS BECAUSE HIS JUDGMENT IS USUALLY BETTER THAN YOUR OWN.

I'M GOING TO SUGGEST YOU SCOOT OUT OF HERE.

I adopted Fidel when I was twenty-three. He's been through a lot of relationship ups and downs with me and is basically a litmus test for potential boyfriends. Take my early twenties, for example. When my longtime crush finally asked me out on a date, I told him I couldn't go because I was busy buying my dog a birthday cake. I did invite him to the birthday party, though, and when he showed up I knew he'd passed the Fidel test.

On the same token, not all guys meet Fidel's high standards. One night after a steamy date, I went to walk the guy out, only to return to my bedroom to find something else steamy—Fidel had pooped on my bed. He's totally housebroken, so it was definitely not an accident. I had to hand it to him for his brutal honesty, and I never saw that guy again.

All said, at the end of the day, I realize that I still love Fidel more than I could love any guy, ever.

Jessica & Fidel
BROOKLYN, NEW YORK ◙ TINYWOLFFACTORY

YOU MAKE SURE THAT YOUR FIRST QUESTION TO THE REALTOR IS, "IS THERE A POOL FOR MY DOG?"

Since my Chihuahuas are my life, I decided that any house we rented or owned had to have a pool. My pups are worth every penny lost to chlorine. With every raft I buy for the pool, I think, "Can Snoop and Diesel use this?"

Lauren, Diesel & Snoop Dogg
PORT ST. LUCIE, FLORIDA DIESEL_SNOOPDOGG

HOUSE FOR SALE!

Looking to sell this BEAUTIFUL two-story home to a happy, deserving dog and his humans. The living room comes furnished with newly upholstered humping surfaces and the carpets have been tastefully marked. The kitchen features low countertops at EXCELLENT scavenging level—PERFECT for snatching food! The home offers three bedrooms, plus upstairs and downstairs drinking fountains. The house also comes with a spacious outdoor bathroom, complete with recently dug-up garden and several shady trees. These trees are the marked territory of the previous owner and are not for sale.

YOU ACCEPT AND LOVE EVERYTHING THAT COMES WITH HAVING A TRASH-LOVING BOOGER FOR A DOG.

Zuke, short for Azuki Bean, is my trash-loving partner in crime. I plan the inventory for BarkBox and accept that he loves trash more than anything we could put in a box. We were once filming a video at the office about whether your dog loves you more than food. When the cameras went on, Zuke walked right past both me and the gigantic, delicious bone on the ground and chose the trash can in the back. I can't blame him for knowing what he likes: he was found eating a moldy Slim Jim as a stray in Oklahoma.

For his first birthday with me, I got him a lamb shank. It was actually hard to think about what to get him because at BarkBox he gets to eat anything he's ever dreamed about. Realizing that the worst thing about his birthday was not knowing how to make his life even *better* was the best feeling as a dog parent.

Patricia & Azuki
NEW YORK, NEW YORK 📷 TINYHYENA

TRASH CAN (\traSH kan\) n.

An AMAZING speakeasy—literally all the tastiest snacks in the world, totally free, if you know where to find it. Sometimes there's a door to get in but—expert tip—you can totally skip the line if you knock it over.

YOU HAVE NO PROBLEM WORKING INTO THE WEE HOURS OF THE NIGHT TO GET THAT PERFECT PICTURE.

I've dedicated hours of my time and spent entire afternoons taking photos to capture my dogs' personalities and tell our story through fun and creative photos. We often venture outdoors to take photos in public locations, where I usually have to grin and bear it as strangers stare my pups down wondering what in the world we're doing!

Emily, Kokoro & Chibi
LOS ANGELES, CALIFORNIA ⬛ EMWNG

SIT (`sit) v.

1. This thing that humans make you do to justify giving you a treat.

2. The easiest thing in the world and somehow they always seem to be impressed.

YOU SPEND HOURS DIGGING YOUR DOG A SNOW RACETRACK AFTER A BLIZZARD.

...and re-digging, and re-digging, and re-digging.

No matter how cold it gets outside, Perrin loves to sprint in a circuit around the perimeter of my yard. So when the snow got to be over her head last winter, I spent hours digging—and then re-digging after each new storm—a trench that she could use as a racetrack. She especially loved the fact that the trench walls served as a great shelf for storing her toys and for getting a good view of the rest of the yard.

Natalie & Perrin
FRAMINGHAM, MASSACHUSETTS 📷 PERRINPUP

Lemon? Banana? Quince? Whatever it is, yellow snow is my favorite flavor!

SNOW (\snö\) n.
A fluffy, seasonal dirt flavor, popular with humans.
Tastiest in yellow.

YOU TRAVEL AND LIVE AS A PACK.

As Minnie and Max's humans, we are in the unique position of sharing them with fans around the world via social media while at the same time trying to be responsible pet owners. Our photos and videos are not elaborate productions. We live a good life but a simple one. Minnie and Max are not spoiled—they get very few treats and virtually no human food, and they sleep on the floor in their own bed.

That said, we are lucky enough to be able to spend more time with our pets than is typical. Daily outings and frequent road trips have become a way of life for them. "Road trip" is part of their vocabulary. If Minnie and Max are at all spoiled, it is because they expect to be a part of almost everything, including our conversations. We travel and live as a pack, and we wouldn't have it any other way...nor would they.

Steve, Minnie & Max
MENLO PARK, CALIFORNIA
🅵 MINNIE & MAX THE PUGS

YOU LET YOUR DOG JOIN THE DOODLE MAFIA.

I knew I wanted to be a Doodle dad, but I didn't want to rush it. Fortunately, just months after our search began, we found our dream Doodle at Animal Haven. As soon as Samson and Hudson, kingpins of the NYC Doodle Mafia, heard we adopted Monty, the Doodle dots aligned—Monty was officially welcomed into the Mafia that weekend.

It takes a certain type of dog owner to be in the Doodle Mafia. Your Doodle becomes part of your social life because there's nothing better than being surrounded by a group of people who are just as crazy about their dogs as you are. Will you carry your fifty-pound Doodle on the subway just so he can enjoy an afternoon in the park? Of *course* you will. Will you drive upstate with a complete stranger who also happens to have a Doodle? Um, is that even a *question*?

We have playdates in the park, hang out at one another's other's apartments, or go to dog-friendly bars and restaurants. We've even talked about going all the way to San Francisco to meet the West Coast Doods and planning a Doodle cruise.

The Doodle Mafia is not just about Instagram likes or followers. It's a very real community of people who are brought together by their love of Doodles. They are the ones who will support your Dood when he gets a bad haircut. Some of us may be Goldendoodles, or Labradoodles, or Bernadoodles, and we may come from all over the world, but at the end of the day we're all one big curly family.

Matt, Marni & Monty
BROOKLYN, NEW YORK MONTYDOODLEDOO

I'M GONNA MAKE YOU A PAWFFER YOU CAN'T REFUSE.

RULES OF THE DOODLE MAFIA

NEVER RAT A DOODLE OUT. If a Doodle poops in the living room, you keep that between you and the rug. Someone's always watching. (Your mom has a puppy cam probably.)

MAKE FRIENDS WITH THE HEAD DOODLES. Follow them on Instagram, go to a Doodle meetup, and then make them a pawffer they can't refuse. (Hint: Bacon.)

YOUR INSTAGRAM HANDLE MUST HAVE THE WORD "DOODLE" IN IT. You're not just a dog. You're a Doodle. Not having "Doodle" in your Instagram handle would be like the Rock saying "Hey, guys, just call me Dwayne." No, Dwayne. You are Dwayne, THE ROCK. And if you were a Doodle you would be @DwayneTheDoodle.

MAINTAIN THAT FLUFF. What is a Doodle without a great head (and body) of curls? NOT a Doodle. Brush your locks so they don't get matted. Condition. And NEVER go for a walk in the rain without a raincoat. A wet Doodle is a sad Doodle, and no one likes a Debbie Doodle.

FIND YOUR TEDDY BEAR. Look, if you want to fool around with other stuffed animals, no one is judging. But at a certain point, you have to realize that Doodles and teddy bears just go together. So find that bear, snuggle the hell out of that thing, and fill the Internet with teddy bear ruvin'. (Fun game: find a teddy bear that fits your exact shade of Doodle and see if people can tell you apart).

BRING YOUR PJS. Every Doodle in the Mafia has a onesie. It's just something you gotta do(odle). If you show up to a slumber pawty and you're not wearing a onesie, it is considered disrespectful.

INSTAGRAM PETIQUETTE. Follow all the Doodles. East Coast, West Coast, around the world, wherever. Tell them how great they look after they get groomed, like their #TBT puppy pics, and compliment them on their side tongue for #tongueouttuesday. Don't start Doodle drama. Also, credit your Doodles.

WEAR SUNGLASSES INDOORS. WEAR DOGGLES ON VESPAS. The sun never sets on a badass, or a Doodle. Goggles are arguably the most difficult accessory to pull off. No one looks cool in them. But of course, #doggledoods come around and make them adorable.

KEEP YOUR DOODLES IN THE LOOP WHEN THERE IS A NEW HASHTAG. When taking a group shot use #SquadGoals. Decide before the meetup: you need to know if it's #pizzaplaidpawty or #pizzapawtyplaid. Whatever the hashtag is, you just do it. You don't question it. If it's #DoodsGetFit, you get your Doodle in a sweatband and bike shorts and you upload that pic. If it's #DoodsGetLit, you wrap some Christmas lights around that Dood and light it up.

DOODS BEFORE DUDES. Don't ditch your Dood to hang out with anyone that is not a Dood.

DON'T START DRAMA. If another dog or breed tries to start drama, FURGETTABOUTIT. Doods just want to get along. Just say the word and we'll put a hit out. (That's an UNFOLLOW, btw.)

YOU MAKE ALL PHONE CALLS BEFORE YOU GET HOME SO YOU CAN SPEND MORE TIME WITH YOUR DOG.

I adopted my dog, Brody Alfonso Dominic, from a shelter. He was found wandering the streets in the aftermath of Hurricane Sandy. Shortly after I brought him home, he caught on to the fact that when I was on the phone, he received less attention. If I, or any houseguests, dare to talk on the phone, Brody barks! My family nicknamed him "Sergeant Brodillini of the Phone Police." I've gotten into the habit of making my calls before I get home so Brody gets my undivided attention!

Tamatha & Brody
RED BANK, NEW JERSEY

YOU NAMED YOUR DOG AFTER YOUR FAVORITE PLACE IN THE ENTIRE WORLD.

While exploring around Buttle Lake in Strathcona Provincial Park, my then-boyfriend and I stumbled upon Myra Falls, a stunning waterfall with an upper and lower viewing point. When we got to the bottom, we were in awe. We lay on the rocks to enjoy the sounds of the cascading water, feeling, in that moment, as if time had stopped. Soon after, my boyfriend asked if we could name our pup after Myra Falls. And we did.

Harper & Myra
BELLEVILLE, ONTARIO 📷 AUSSIEOVERLOAD

YOU SELL YOUR HOUSE TO PAY FOR YOUR DOG'S BACK SURGERY.

Yes, it's true, and I would do it again.

Kim & Dottie
RUSSELLVILLE, ARKANSAS 📷 DOTTIEDOXIE

YOU GIVE YOUR DOG THE BEST FLOATIES IN THE POOL—EVEN THOUGH HE CONTINUES TO POP THEM.

King Bentley pops about one pool floatie per month during the summer. He loves to float on them in the pool, but when he sees them lying in the grass, he thinks they are toys and charges at them. He tries to drag the floatie in his mouth, like a giant, floating dog bed, deflating it slowly until it's flat as a pancake. Then he sits next to it and stares up at us with a confused look on his face. Even though this same thing continues to happen over and over, our family loves him, and will keep buying him floaties so he can keep popping them to his heart's content!

Lexie & King Bentley
NEW YORK, NEW YORK 📷 KINGBENTLEYTHEBULLDOG

YOU KEEP A METICULOUS LAUNDRY LIST OF ALL OF YOUR DOG'S FORMER LOVES—AND LOSSES.

Dacia & Ruby Roo
LOS ANGELES, CALIFORNIA 📷 MS_RUBY_ROO

A Eulogy for Fallen Toys

You and your other furry, stuffed, wooden, squeaky, woven, and painted buddies have all met the same unfortunate fate over the past nine months: a chew session with Ms. Ruby Roo. As her parents, we know she really loved you—all of you. She would throw you in the air, jump on you like a wolf in the snow looking for a mouse, and would always show you off to the dogs next door. You are the unsung heroes that kept our girl happy and let her experience a joy that was denied from her as a pup. A vibrant chorus of ripping and squeaking sounds that were mere fantasies as she recovered from being hit by a car with three broken bones at the shelter, as she stayed with foster families, and as she eagerly awaited a family to give her love. To honor you, we keep a list; a running reminder of things she has loved. You are her memories, and you will not be forgotten.

- Mr. Ducky
- Squid
- 1 large wobbly treat dispenser
- 1 set of "invincible" rubber chains
- Ladybug pillow
- Banana (pronounced) Bah-nah-nah
- 2 freezer chew toys
- 2 "indestructible" chew toys
- Snake squeaker
- Blue squeaky dog
- Halloween ghost squeaker
- Sir Hedgehog
- Rubber toy tire
- Red squiggly squeaker
- Squeaky orange bone
- 1 water hose
- 1 pencil sharpener
- 2 sets of water sprinkler systems
- Donut squeak
- 2 pairs of shoe insoles
- 1 bath mat
- 2 outside mats
- 6 ropes
- 8 tennis balls
- 3 dog beds
- 2 kiddie pools
- 1 ottoman
- 1 toy basket
- 3 hair ties
- 1 dress
- Set of clips on a vest
- 2 long leashes
- 1 pair of high heels
- 3 pairs of flip-flops
- 1 bra
- 1 small throw pillow
- 1 large husband pillow
- the wall

TOY ADDICTION

Pimm:
Hello. My name is Pimm.

Group:
Hiiii, Pimm.

Pimm:
It has been three weeks since my last squeakhillation, on my pawnor, or may I wear the cone of shame for eternity.

[Group applauds]

Dog 1:
You're an inspiration to us all!

Dog 2:
Amen!

YOU BLOW YOUR ENTERTAINMENT BUDGET ON DOG TOYS.

I found myself constantly browsing online or going to the pet store when my husband and I first got Chompers. Since he was our first pup, we weren't sure what to expect, so we tried a little of everything: furry toys, squeaky toys, toys without stuffing, and so on. Before we knew it, he had a huge assortment of toys and there were *always* more on the way. He's also had BarkBox since he was less than a year old, so there were always new toys and treats to look forward to every month.

He now has at least three full bins of toys, even after paring down over the years. And ever since he learned how to play fetch, he's been obsessed with squeaky balls! As a result, we are always well stocked with them in the house.

Katie & Chompers
SAN FRANCISCO, CALIFORNIA
◎ CHOMPERSTHECORGI

YOU DON'T MIND HAVING A FULL TOY BOX IN THE CENTER OF YOUR HOUSE.

Ruckus is a hoarder of all good things in our house. He even has his own room and storage space! We used to trip over his toys all over the house, but now he does a good job of cleaning up by returning them to his toy bin, which lives in the center of the family room! And yes, he knows the trick of "cleaning up," aka picking up his toys and placing them back in his bin on request.

Family & Ruckus
SILICON VALLEY, CALIFORNIA  RUCKUSTHEESKIE

YOU ARE GUILTY OF SPOILING YOUR DOG.

We spoil Ellie because she's one of a kind! Have you seen her looks? With the pure Lab head and the questionable body, she looks more like a cow than anything—and that's why we love her.

Julie & Ellie
COON RAPIDS, MINNESOTA 📷 THEMUTTLIFE

YOU SLEEP IN A VET EMERGENCY ROOM ALL NIGHT WAITING FOR YOUR DOG TO WAKE UP.

When Stanley was bitten by another dog in the middle of the night, I took him straight to the emergency room. He would have to be sedated to have his ear stitched up, and the vet thought it would be best if I picked him up the next morning. Instead, I decided to stay the night in the waiting room so Stanley wouldn't have to wake up alone in a crate. I wanted to be by his side so he would know that everything would be better soon.

I fell asleep in my chair, and at around four a.m. the door to the waiting room opened and Stanley stumbled through the door with his "cone of fame" hitting the door frame. I was very excited to see that everything went well and that, despite being pretty dopey from the drugs, Stanley was still happy to see me.

Donald & Stanley
TORONTO, ONTARIO  SCHNAUZERSTANLEY

I'LL BITE YOUR STITCHES IF YOU'LL BITE MINE...

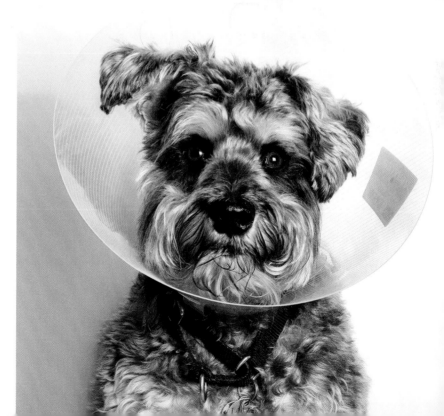

YOU ADD A NEW PUP TO THE FAMILY TO MAKE YOUR SENIOR DOG FEEL 140 DOG YEARS YOUNGER.

On February 14, 2000, we rescued five-year-old Sully. He was confused, damaged, and terrified. He feared men, ropes, belts, and scarves. His fear manifested itself as naughtiness and destructiveness.

After a week of coping with Sully's demanding and draining behavior, I made the difficult decision to return him to the rescue. When the rescue volunteer arrived to collect him, he shared that Sully had already been returned from three homes and had little chance of being rescued again. As Sully was

Nowadays, you puppies get soft, chewy treats! We chewed on rocks and it made us STRONGER.

being led away, I suddenly couldn't let him go. I had to give him another chance. From that moment on, he was a different dog. It was almost like he understood what happened.

Nearly a decade later, fourteen-year-old Sully lost Annie, his partner. He was devastated, and nothing we did could improve his mood. The vet insisted he would forget after a few weeks, but when weeks turned into months, we decided to get another playmate for him. Along came HoneyB the Miniature Labradoodle, Sully's magic medicine. His love for life returned. Although he is losing his sight and hearing, has Addison's disease, and had a toe removed, twenty-year-old Sully still runs with the youngsters! His story serves as a beautiful reminder that all dogs deserve a chance at happiness and love.

Gill, Sully, HoneyB & BumbleB
LANCASHIRE, UNITED KINGDOM
HONEYB_DOODLE

SEVEN REASONS YOU SHOULD ADOPT A SENIOR DOG

➕ Senior dogs tend to be less inclined to go for long walks and would rather be either in your arms or cuddled up next to you on the couch. These are wonderful things.

➕ Senior dogs have a lifetime's worth of personality to give you, which makes every day extra exciting/adventurous/hilarious.

➕ Learning a senior dog's behavior teaches you a lot about yourself! For example: if a senior dog still goes crazy when presented with a spoon of peanut butter, you should feel comfortable having the same reaction regardless of your age.

➕ Senior dogs are incredibly photogenic (read: they move less, thus making them easier to capture in a photo).

➕ Senior dogs need homes just as badly as any other dog, yet they get overlooked constantly.

➕ Most likely your senior dog will already be house trained and know some tricks! Imagine: sit, stay, and "do you have to go potty?" all meaning something on day one!

➕ Senior dogs are much more calm and tend to be better with people and other dogs right off the bat!

D'YOU WANNA TELL THE NEW GUY HE'S ADOPTED OR SHOULD I?

PERFORMANCE REVIEW FROM YOUR DOG

	1	2	3	4	5
Personality					
Willingness to learn new tricks			X		
Willingness to accept feedback			X		
Willingness to share food	X				
Willingness to give up social life					X
Shows perpetual interest in work (me)					X
Follows instructions fully		X			
Neat and tidy in appearance	X				
Skills (during walks, mealtime, bedtime, cuddle schedule)					
Consistent and quality belly-rubs-per-minute (BPM) rate				X	
Requires minimal supervision	X				
Treats available on command		X			
Punctuality				X	
Problem solving ability			X		
Creativity			X		
Dependability					X

Comments

* TREAT ACQUISITION AND DISTRIBUTION REQUIRES A DRAMATIC INCREASE.

* GAMES OF FETCH ARE CURRENTLY AVERAGING 3.5 THROWS PER SESSION. LET'S BUMP THAT UP TO 119.

* THE TEAM SHOULD BE EATING 20 PERCENT MORE RANDOM THINGS OFF THE GROUND. I'M WILLING TO LEAD ON THIS ONE.

* HEAD-PAT-TO-BELLY-RUB CONVERSION RATES ARE STAGNATING (40 PERCENT). LET'S AIM FOR 75 PERCENT.

* LET'S EXPAND OUR REACH—THERE ARE EMERGING PROPERTIES JUST WAITING TO BE MARKED, LIKE THE GOOD COUCH.

1 - Poor   2 - Adequate   3 - Good   4 - Very Good   5 - Excellent

YOU KNOW WHEN YOUR DOG IS YOUR BOSS.

I don't say I walk my dogs because that suggests I have control over them. I accompany them on their walks. Corgnelius is the heavier of my two Corgis, weighing about fifty pounds, so when he wants to stop walking, he stops. And I don't mean he begrudgingly slows down and struggles against his leash like a normal dog—he stops moving and drops to the floor. One time he dead stopped in front of a garage as a car pulled up to go inside. I had to drag him excruciatingly slowly out of the way so the driver could get in. Believe me, a fifty-pound dog feels like five hundred pounds when there's a pair of angry eyes glaring at you!

Susan, Corgnelius & Stumphrey
LOS ANGELES, CALIFORNIA ☉ CORGNELIUS

YOU TOLD THE STORY OF HOW YOU STALKED A CELEBRITY DOG SO FREQUENTLY THAT IT BROUGHT YOU YOUR OWN CELEBRITY DOG.

My time with Noodle all began because of my obsession with HRH Doug the Pug. Last year I went on an epic quest to meet Doug, which proved successful after a change.org campaign, a handful of excitement-induced blackouts, and a very understanding Mother Doug, and we have maintained a healthy relationship ever since. I often tell the harrowing tale of how I—a simple homosexual from upstate New York with a flair for karaoke and wool socks—came to meet Doug the Pug at various stand-up places across the city. One night after a set, a woman approached me and said she had a seven-and-a-half-year-old pug named Noodle who needed a home and insisted that our "spirits were perfect together." When we met, he was as glorious as the sun, with each fold being more luxurious than the last. That's the end of the story and the start of our perfect life together.

Jonathan & Noodle
HARLEM, NEW YORK ◉ SHOWMENOODZ

FASHION

(faSHen) n.

An unnecessary form of torture in which your human attempts to destroy your canine street cred by placing your body into ridiculous accessories such as hats, glasses, onesies, dresses, and sweaters, and then expects you to look like you are enjoying yourself on camera. I'm just in it for the treats.

YOU SPEND MORE TIME ON YOUR DOG'S HALLOWEEN COSTUME THAN YOUR OWN.

I spent hours making Dottie a *Star Wars* costume because none of the store-bought ones fit her. I'm also convinced that my dog is cuter than any kid dressed up on Halloween.

Kim & Dottie
RUSSELLVILLE, ARKANSAS 🔘 DOTTIEDOXIE

YOU REALIZE THAT LIFE IS TOO SHORT TO WEAR BORING CLOTHES. . . THANKS TO YOUR DOG.

The French poet Anatole France wrote, "Until one has loved an animal, a part of one's soul remains unawakened." Maya came into my life when I was dealing with a death in the family. Through her devotion, selflessness, and unfaltering optimism, Maya brought hope and grace to a very dark time. She makes me a better person as I strive to be worthy of such love and loyalty. She has truly awoken a part of my soul. She also taught me that life is too short to wear boring clothes.

Tania & Maya
LOS ANGELES, CALIFORNIA ◉ MAYA_ON_THE_MOVE

YOU ACCEPT THAT YOUR DOG'S WARDROBE IS BIGGER THAN YOUR OWN.

When I first adopted Chloe I bought exactly two orange fleece shirts for her to wear. I swore I would never be one of those people who dressed their dog. Everyone said, "Just wait," and I would say, "Oh no, I would never." But working at Martha Stewart (home to Martha Stewart Pets), I admit—I got sucked in. These clothes are the size of my hand! How can I not turn to mush over them?

Dorie & Chloe Kardoggian
NEW YORK, NEW YORK ⓘ CHLOEKARDOGGIAN

PUREWOW NAMED HER MOST FASHIONABLE DOG OF THE YEAR FOR 2015

YOU KNOW THAT YOUR DOG HAS A BETTER SENSE OF STYLE THAN YOU.

As Toby's personal stylist, I'm always on the lookout for new pieces to add to his wardrobe. Toby's style is a combination of "hipster meets dapper dude" with a side of attitude. A typical OOTD (Outfit of the Day) would be a plaid shirt, bow tie, fedora, and his signature thick-rimmed glasses. Pants aren't a priority in Toby's closet—he finds them way too restrictive! It's not always easy buying clothes to fit a nine-pound hipster, but there's a thrill that comes with finding something that fits both Toby's size and style. I do most of my shopping online since it's quite funny explaining to a sales associate that I'm shopping for a ten-year-old boy who's nine pounds and ten inches tall!

Joyce & Toby Little Dude
VANCOUVER, CANADA TOBY_LITTLEDUDE

YOU HIRED A PERSONAL TAILOR FOR YOUR DOG.

Koki is a rescued Shih Tzu with an old soul and a big heart. Each night, he shares a glimpse of his happy life in NYC on Instagram with the Empire State Building as his backdrop. In a show of solidarity and support, Koki wears clothes that match the color of the Empire State Building every evening to promote and raise awareness for a variety of causes, events, and special celebrations. Our family members in India source specialty fabric and have a tailor custom-make Koki's Indian-inspired kurtas. Koki's wardrobe is more diverse than both of ours combined.

Vijay, Hector & Koki
NEW YORK, NEW YORK 📷 KOKISTATEOFMIND

YOU'D BETTER NOT BE GETTING INTO MY STUFF AGAIN...

YOU HAD YOUR DOG MODEL FOR A BARNEYS AD CAMPAIGN.

Lulu is a true New Yorker who resides on the Lower East Side. The neighborhood is filled with small shops that she loves to visit on our daily walks. She even recognizes her favorite cafés and insists that we stop in! She also adores our adventures to the Upper East Side, especially when we stop at Bergdorf Goodman's shoe department. On one occasion, she even got kisses from Manolo Blahnik himself! Oh, and did I mention she was in a Barneys ad campaign?

Heidi & Lulu
NEW YORK, NEW YORK 📷 LULUNASTY

YOU HAPPILY ACCEPT THAT YOUR DOG IS A DIVA.

We never quite know what my diva—who follows her passion for fashion—might need, so we typically bring everything so she's always prepared. She normally looks better than most of us do.

Diane & Sparkles
ALPHARETTA, GEORGIA ◉ SPARKLESTHEDIVA

QUIZ: WHAT DOES YOUR DOG'S FASHION SAY ABOUT YOU?

In the winter, your dog is most likely to wear...

A. The latest fashion, straight from the most sophisticated dog parks of Paris.

B. A cute jacket-and-sweater combo. Wore it last season but it's still good!

C. Nothing. My dog would only wear a jacket if it was really cold and they actually needed it.

Does your dog wear booties?

A. Yes. Duh. Always.

B. Sometimes.

C. Do booties cover the dog's butt or, like, paws?

Does your dog's favorite harness match your favorite bag or does it _match_-match your favorite bag?

A. It usually matches my favorite bag. It only _match_-matches if we're trying to be ironic.

B. If they match, that's a cool coincidence, but it'd be unintentional.

C. Wait, why are you guys saying "_match_-match"?

Does your dog have a raincoat?

A. What? No. They have _several_ raincoats. Is this a trick question?

B. Yes, they have a raincoat.

C. No, my dog's fine just being naked in the rain.

On a scale of Chihuahua to Great Dane (very small to very large), how big a fashion statement can the right collar make?

A. Great Dane. Every part of every outfit matters.

B. Somewhere between a Chihuahua and a Great Dane, so like some kind of spaniel, I guess?

C. What do you mean by "right" collar? A collar just needs to fit my dog's neck, correct?

When is the last time you were inspired by a great dog fashion idea on Pinterest?

A. I'm on Pinterest right now.

B. I've probably done it once or twice.

C. I don't think I ever have.

Have you ever considered quitting your current job to become a professional dog fashion designer?

A. Yes. In fact I did and I am now a professional pup designer.

B. Ha ha, no... but I bet it'd be fun.

C. Dog fashion designer? Is that a thing?

Finish this sentence: "My dog's fashion is...

A. "...everything."

B. "...something fun to splurge on every now and then."

C. "...look, I'm obviously option C, okay?"

If you answered mostly A's, you're a...

FULL-BLOWN FASHIONISTA!

You and your pup are quite the haute couture pair. You two are always in on the latest trends, and your head-turning style is constantly stopping people—and pups—in their tracks. You're both always dressed to impress, from head to paw to toe. If your dog doesn't have an Instagram account yet, you should start one today—your fans are waiting to see more of you and your pup's fearless style!

If you answered mostly B's, you're a...

CLASSIC FASHIONISTA!

While you and your dog don't live for fashion, you certainly appreciate it. You enjoy a good splurge every now and then, but for the most part, you and your pup stick to classic pieces that are popular *and* practical.

If you answered mostly C's, you're a...

RATIONALISTA!

You're not interested in the latest trends, but you're fine with that. You and your dog are more likely to be found chilling on the couch or enjoying a walk than perusing Pinterest pages or shopping for the latest booties (which, for the record, are for a dog's feet, not their butt). If and when you do style your dog, it's only when there's a clear, rational purpose behind it—like keeping your pup warm during the winter. Take the money you save not buying clothes and plan a fun trip for you and your four-legged friend!

YOU BECOME A DOG CHEF SO 100 PERCENT OF YOUR LIFE IS DEDICATED TO YOUR PUPS.

My husband and I started 2 Traveling Dogs in 2011 when we moved across the country with our two rescue dogs, Peanut Butter Brickle and Digby Pancake. The blog's purpose was to show everyone how to safely move with dogs. We quickly learned that Brickle and Digby's personalities resonated with others when their Facebook fan base exploded in a matter of weeks (it's now over 1 million followers!). We wanted to do something meaningful with their newfound fame; unsurprisingly, rescue dogs became our mission. Every day, we share images of dogs who have twenty-four hours or less to live before a shelter euthanizes them.

After the blog's success and the resulting popularity on Facebook, our lives became "everything dog." When Brickle started having health issues, we threw away our dog food bags and headed to the kitchen to try our hands at being dog chefs. Within two weeks, his problems were gone! Our loyal fans wanted our recipes and we desperately wanted to help other dogs get healthy. As the demand increased, we

decided to quit our corporate jobs and make a go of the dog treat business. Since then, we have never looked back. In 2012, we launched Your Dog's Diner, a line of mixes that pup parents can whip up in their own kitchen by adding a few simple ingredients like fresh meat and eggs. Brickle and Digby are the company's quality control officers!

Rachael, Nathan, Brickle & Digby
LUTZ, FLORIDA 2 TRAVELING DOGS

BARKARITAS!

INGREDIENTS

- 1½ cups unsalted turkey, chicken, or beef broth
- 1 cup frozen, seedless watermelon cubes
- 2 tablespoons honey
- 2 tablespoons unsweetened shredded coconut
- Turkey bacon bits for rim

Optional, additional garnishes:
- Fresh mint
- A slice of cantaloupe or honeydew melon
- 1 slice cooked turkey bacon

DIRECTIONS

1. Pour the broth into an ice cube tray. Freeze the broth and the watermelon cubes for at least 2 hours.

2. Remove the frozen broth and watermelon from freezer. Put them into a blender. Pulse until they reach the desired consistency.

3. Dip the rim of a bowl or glass into the honey, then into the coconut and bacon bits.

4. Garnish with fresh mint, a slice of melon, or a slice of turkey bacon!

Optional:
All dogs needs pup chips with their barkarita! Serve with dehydrated sweet potato chips and unsweetened yogurt as a dip!

DIGBY & BRICKLE'S FAVE HOMEMADE DEHYDRATED CHICKEN JERKY TREATS FOR DOGS

INGREDIENTS

- 1 pound boneless, skinless chicken breast tenders (partially frozen makes them easier to slice)
- ¼ cup vegetable oil
- Juice of one lemon
- 2 tablespoons honey
- Your choice of dog-friendly seasonings: parsley, rosemary, sage (preferably fresh and chopped very fine)

DIRECTIONS

1. Rinse the chicken breasts and remove any fat, which slows down the dehydrating process and will shorten the jerky's shelf life. Fat may also go rancid quickly in the dehydrator.

2. Slice the chicken into strips about ⅛ to ¼ inch thick, slicing with the grain. This will make the treats chewier!

3. Coat the strips with the oil, lemon juice, honey, and seasonings. Put them in a resealable bag and let them marinate overnight.

4. Place the strips on dehydrator trays, spacing them evenly; make sure they do not touch. The drying process depends on adequate airflow between the strips.

5. Put the trays in the dehydrator, turn it on, and set the temperature for 140 degrees F.

6. It will take between three and twelve hours for the strips to fully dry, depending on how you cut the chicken and the dehydrator settings. To determine the dryness level, remove one strip from the dehydrator, cut into it with a sharp knife, and examine the inside. When the meat is completely dried, there will not be any moisture and it will be the same color throughout. If it needs more time, put it back in! Keep checking until the chicken is dry but not brittle.

7. When your chicken jerky is done, store it in airtight containers or resealable bags. Refrigerate the containers for an even longer shelf life. Safety first!

Note: If you do not have a dehydrator, follow the preceding directions, using an oven set at 200 degrees F.

YOU TRADED IN YOUR CAR FOR ONE THAT MAKES IT EASIER FOR YOU TO TRAVEL WITH YOUR DOG.

We bought this car with Wally in mind. We have dubbed it the Corgmobile where life is simple: Keep Calm and Corgi On.

Marc, Cynthia & Wally
WHARTON, NEW JERSEY
WALLYTHEWELSHCORGI

YOU BRAVE THE BITTER CANADIAN WINTER SO YOUR DOG CAN ROMP IN THE SNOW.

Winter is Oakley's favorite season. She will stay outside until her chest is covered in icicles, and we have to force her inside for a fireplace break.

Rachel, Sylina & Oakley
LONDON, ONTARIO ⬚ OAKLEY_AUSSIE

JACKET (ja-ket) n.
Fuzzy capes that you have to wear when the stuff that's in your water bowl starts falling from the sky.

YOU VIEW YOUR DOG AS A FURRY FORM OF THERAPY.

My Bullmastiff had died in my arms the year before my twin daughters brought a new dog home for Christmas. My husband and I thought we were not ready to love another dog until I held Miller for the first time. I have PTSD, anxiety, and major depression, but having Miller around makes me smile and laugh. Our whole family enjoys how silly he is and how such a big Rottweiler insists on being a lap dog.

Carrie & Miller
GOODYEAR, ARIZONA ⓥ MILLER THE ROTTWEILER

YOU ALWAYS KEEP THE THERMOSTAT IN YOUR HOUSE SET TO "DOG."

Apparently, "dog" is exactly 71 degrees. Our home thermostat never drops one degree below to make sure the boys are sleeping comfortably all day.

Kati, Kevin, Spud & Lunchbox
BERKLEY, MICHIGAN SPUDANDLUNCHBOX

YOU DRIVE TWENTY MILES EVERY WEEK TO BUY YOUR PUP HIS FAVORITE CUPCAKES.

Ninja is a Sprinkles Cupcakes addict! I drive twenty-plus miles once a week to spend $2.50 on each cupcake for him, and at this point, he even knows how to find the door to Sprinkles once we arrive at the outdoor plaza. This all started when Ninja injured his back, so the vet prescribed him six weeks of crate rest. I came up with the idea that with each week he completed crate rest, he would get that number (of weeks) in cupcakes. So by week six when he completed his crate rest, he got six cupcakes!

Cindy & Ninja
SAN JOSE, CALIFORNIA 	 NINJEEEE

YOU WERE WILLING TO BE HOMELESS FOR YOUR DOGS.

I have five animals in my family including a cat, a rabbit, and three dogs—a Chihuahua named Philli (Cheeser), a Collie named Wizard, and a black Lab/American Bulldog mix named Axel (Mr. or Mr. Man). I would do anything for my furry family, and recently, that meant being temporarily homeless. I had no place to live, and finding a rental that would accept me and all my animals proved difficult. People told me to give them away, but splitting up my family was simply not an option.

For the interim period that we tried to find a place to live, we had no place to stay. My grandmother offered us a camper on her property as a temporary home. We lived in that closely confined space for four months, from July until October, and in the summer, the heat was often unbearable. We lost power frequently and water occasionally. By the time fall came, it was hard to keep warm in the near-freezing temperatures. Fortunately, before winter arrived, we found ourselves back in a house. My animals love their new home, especially the big fenced backyard. As I look back on those months living in flux, it was certainly a struggle, but I know I made the right choice. It wouldn't have been home without all of my animals.

Jess, Axel, Wizard & Cheeser
WIND GAP, PENNSYLVANIA

HOME IS EVERYWHERE MY DOGS ARE.

YOU SHARE A BEDROOM WITH YOUR SISTER SO YOUR DOGS CAN HAVE THEIR OWN ROOM.

I live in a medium-sized house in the country with my beautiful Dobermans, Athena Kiara and Blue Deuce. One day, my family and I agreed that the large dog crates were taking up too much room. The only other place we could store the crates was in an outside workshop— and there was *no* way my dogs were going out in the cold! So naturally, my sister and I had our rooms remodeled. She got a larger bed and I gave my room to Athena and Blue Deuce. My dogs have their own newly upgraded space to sleep and I share a room with my sister because that's what real crazy love is.

Taylor, Athena & Blue Deuce
NICHOLS, SOUTH CAROLINA 📷 DOBERMANDUO

YOU GIVE YOUR PUP HIS OWN INTERSPECIES MINI-ME SO HE CAN EXPERIENCE THE SAME JOY YOU FEEL.

We were at the pet store one day and came across a little hamster that looked a lot like Loki. We thought Loki would enjoy her company, so we brought her home! At first, he was a bit cautious, but he warmed up to her soon after. Today, Loki is often seen following Ham-Ham around and giving her boosts up the stairs. Their massive difference in size is definitely not a barrier for their unique friendship!

Tim, Viv & Loki
VANCOUVER, BRITISH COLUMBIA
LOKISTAGRAM LOKIS_HAMSTER

YOU BACKPACKED EIGHT MILES INTO A FOREST TO KEEP YOUR DOGS AS FAR FROM FIREWORKS AS POSSIBLE.

There's nothing my dogs, Fidel and Tito, hate more than fireworks. For the entire month of July, the firecrackers going off in the neighborhood sent them running into the bathroom, hiding and trembling in sheer terror. I knew the big fireworks show on the Fourth of July would be more than they could handle, so I put a plan in place. We loaded up our tent, sleeping bags, and supplies for a campfire feast and backpacked eight miles into the Angeles National Forest so we'd be safely out of earshot of fireworks. That year we didn't enjoy parties and barbecues with friends like normal people, but the sacrifice was worth it to see the dogs having the time of their life, oblivious to the chaos of the city below.

Jess, Warren, Fidel & Tito
BROOKLYN, NEW YORK ☉ TINYWOLFFACTORY

YOU LEARNED FROM YOUR DOG THAT A DISABILITY DOESN'T HAVE TO BE A HANDICAP.

My Chihuahua TurboRoo was born without front legs and spent the beginning of his life hobbling where he could. We first met when he was brought into the clinic where I was a vet tech. I had a soft spot for the animals who needed a little extra help, and at only four weeks old, TurboRoo stole my heart. I knew that I could change his life. What I never expected was that almost a year later that little bundle of fur would lead me to quit my job, become a Dog-Momager, start an amazing company, and now own a charity!

I remember the first time Turbo jumped on the couch as a puppy—it was an amazing feat! For most dogs it is an everyday thing, but it is a huge milestone when you only have two legs, both in the back. Even today, I look over from time to time and catch him jumping on the furniture and can't help reminding myself that *wow, he only has two legs!* Sometimes I forget.

I remember getting a letter when Turbo was just a pup from a woman who had suffered a massive stroke; she had actually sent Turbo a gift from her hospital bed. It was unbelievable to see how one little dog could receive so much love and support from people all over the world for so many different reasons!

Ashley & TurboRoo
SPEEDWAY, INDIANA ☉ TURBOROO

DOG PAWSTHETICS

Turbo's first set of wheels were made from Legos and Tinkertoys and gave him the mobility he so desperately sought. Shortly after, Turbo received his first set of 3D-printed wheels! We knew that Turbo's amazing 3D-printed cart could help others like him, so we decided to create TurboRoo Designs, LLC, to give disabled dogs a chance at a happy four-legged life. Since the company's start in late November 2014, we have fitted over thirty dogs with our carts.

We have since updated the design and plan on continuing to create new designs for specific cases of dogs with front leg deformities.

We also have a new charity called Pawsthetics to make this amazing technology available across the globe for animals who need life-changing prosthetics!

ROO'S ANGELS

YOU SPEND FIVE DAYS MAKING A WAMPA COSTUME FOR YOUR PUG.

My husband and I met because of our love of *Star Wars* and making *Star Wars* costumes, so it seemed quite logical for us to make them for Chubbs. She's a Pug and it's hard to fit her into anything. We knew any outfits that were store-bought were just not going to have the kind of accuracy we would want. Thus, the Wampug was born. It took five days and about $20 to make. What soon followed was Banthapug, which took about two months and some expensive monster fur to create. Then, the Gamorrean Pug guard, which took nine months to make (my most labor-intensive costume for Chubbs to date). And finally, most recently, Kylo Ren, our most expensive costume for Chubbs thanks to 3D modeling and printing of a custom-made helmet sized and shaped specifically to fit her head perfectly, and a custom-sized lightsaber.

Kristen & Chubbs
KINGMAN, ARIZONA
 CHUBBS THE WAMPUG

HOW TO MAKE THE PERFECT OUTFIT FOR YOUR DOG

💩 Think about your dog's body type, personality, and lifestyle and choose to make something that would complement him. This should not only be fun for you, but for your dog too!

💩 Look for patterns online or in a pattern book. I found a wonderful book on knitting dog sweaters!

💩 Get a dog mannequin. Believe it or not, these are becoming easier to find and are very helpful since they don't move around like your pet does.

💩 Make a mockup of the outfit out of muslin first. This can save you from making a mistake with your good fabric.

💩 Keep trying your mockup on your pet, make adjustments, then try it on again prior to making the final pieces out of your good fabric. Make sure the fit is comfortable and safe and allows for proper movement.

KRISTEN, MOTHER OF CHUBBS

YOU DRIVE TO A DIFFERENT STATE TO FIND THE PERFECT SOMBRERO FOR YOUR DOG.

I love finding just the right outfits for certain occasions for my little Frenchies. Once, I even drove an hour to a swap meet to find the perfect sombrero for my Frenchie Frank for Cinco de Mayo, and then had my niece make a poncho out of a placemat.

Angela, Myra, Doris, Lola & Frank
ROSEMOUNT, MINNESOTA
📷 THREELITTLEFRENCHIES

YOU CHASED AFTER A STRANGER IN THE RAIN TO SEE IF YOUR DOGS MIGHT BE TWINS...

KRISTEN, PIG'S MOM

I always wonder about my rescue dog's past. Where is she from? Who are her parents? Where are her siblings? My dog Pig is (supposedly) a Shih Tzu/Pit Bull/Frenchie mix with wiry white hair, a ballerina stance, and an old man face. I was driving home from work one day when I saw someone walking a dog that looked just like my dog. I pulled over, went up to the owner, and showed her a photo of Pig. She was as excited as I was because we both knew our dogs were sisters.

At the park, our dogs rolled in the mud the same way, walked the same, barked the same, and had the same full-on meltdown at the sight of a squirrel. There's no doubt they're twin sisters. Even if it turns out my dog is the evil twin, I love her just the same! Over the next few weeks, we texted each other a million dog photos, and when it finally turned nice, we set up a playdate.

Kristen & Pig
BROOKLYN, NEW YORK
SHEDBROOKLYN

...AND THEN PUT THEM ON A PLAYDATE.

MARGARET, MILLIE'S MOM

I've spent hours in front of my computer trying to find pictures of dogs that look like my dog, Millie. According to her adoption papers, she is a Jack Russell and pit bull mix, but none of the dogs I found online had Millie's physical features. One day, a woman came up to me while I was walking Millie and told me she had pulled her car over to talk to me because her dog looked just like my dog. When she showed me pictures of her dog, I knew at once that they must be sisters. They had the same wiry mane, brown whiskers, blocky head, and sausage body.

Millie and Pig have had two playdates. They have the exact same hopping run, love mulching sticks, and lie down with their back legs splayed out like frogs. I still can't believe how amazing it is that they found one another. Kristen thinks Pig is Millie's evil twin because Pig pees in the shower and eats garbage. While Millie doesn't pee in the shower, she definitely loves eating chicken bones she finds on the street. I think they're both angels.

Margaret & Millie
BROOKLYN, NEW YORK
📷 MARGARSTEVENS

YOU BATHE 235 POUNDS OF DOG LIKE IT'S NO BIG DEAL.

We're so crazy about our dogs, Finn and Gemma, that we're willing to bathe both of them—a collective 235 pounds!—on a regular basis. But it's no simple wash-and-go. It takes squeaky toys to lure them in, a swimsuit (no matter the season) to keep from ruining clothes, and ibuprofen in case your back bends a little too far forward. And shampoo. Lots of shampoo.

Camille, Richard, Finn & Gemma
JERSEY CITY, NEW JERSEY

WHAT, NO CONDITIONER?

DOG SHAMPOO

TIPS FROM THE EXPERT: DIRECTIONS FOR WASHING AN XL DOG

STEP 1
Soap up and scrub in sections, like a butcher's beef chart—neck, leg, flank, rump.

STEP 2
Pay close attention to the wrinkles—like your couch, you might find change in there if you look hard enough.

STEP 3
Rinse again and again and again because you probably missed a spot.

BY CAMILLE, MOTHER OF FINN & GEMMA

YOU MAKE SURE THE DECOR IN YOUR HOME IS DESIGNED TO COMPLEMENT YOUR DOG'S CRIB.

Our very first apartment was decorated in an inexpensive modern-Ikea style when along came Carl and his amazing custom-built dog house. It had been constructed of reclaimed barn wood and had wallpaper, built-in lighting, and a corrugated metal roof. Since Carl's house was much nicer than ours, we had to ensure that all of our future furniture and decor complemented his. Our home is now fully "Carl-chic."

Jon, Alex & Carl
SANTA ROSA, CALIFORNIA 📷 CARL.THE.DOG

IT'S A DUPLEX.

STEP 4
Let 'em jump out of the tub and stand back as they shake it all off. (How the inside of the closed medicine cabinet gets wet is anyone's guess.)

STEP 5
Towel them off, then convince yourself that they're dry even though you know you'll find wet spots anywhere they lie down in the next three hours.

STEP 6
Now that Dog #1 is done, repeat as needed for consecutive dogs.

STEP 7
After you clear all the hair from the tub and mop up every inch of the bathroom, sit down, stay, and give *yourself* a treat.

YOU BUY A NEW BAG AND THE FIRST QUESTION THAT POPS INTO YOUR HEAD IS "WILL MY DOG BE COMFORTABLE AND LOOK CUTE IN THIS?"

WHAT'S IN MERVIN'S BAG?

Poop Bag

Anna Karenina

Fluff Remnants

Toothbrush to Clean Tongue

Searching for the perfect bag takes time, especially when you factor in your dog's happiness, comfort, and coolness. My favorite bag to carry him in is a green bag from Filson because it's sturdy and the perfect shape. I always make sure to put a comfy blanket in the bottom and carry it over my shoulder so he has a great view of the world. People always take pictures of him when I carry him in this bag.

My pups can also recognize the difference between my work bag and other bags. When I use one of my personal bags, I have to hide it and sneak it out of the apartment; otherwise they start crying. If I were to leave it on the ground they would automatically jump into it.

Joey & Mervin
NEW YORK, NEW YORK 📷 MERVINTHECHIHUAHUA

YOU KNOW YOU DON'T HAVE TO BE A PERFECT PERSON TO BE A PERFECT PARENT.

I fell in love with my first foster dog, Lola, immediately upon meeting her. Even so, I never thought I could have my own dog. I had a tiny city apartment and I wasn't sure if I could deal with the responsibility. I was set on finding her a home that was as loving as mine had been for my childhood dog. I wanted Lola to have kids to grow with, a house, a big backyard; I wanted her to find the perfect life.

I took her to adoption events, but whenever I did, she would sit on my lap and snarl at anyone who approached us. One day at the dog park, I saw a bus sign with a picture of a child and a parent that read, "You don't have to be a perfect person to be a perfect parent." It was a sign for human adoption, but that was when something clicked in my head. I realized my love for Lola was perfect and better than a love that anyone could give her. She didn't need a perfect family life; she needed someone who loves her like I do.

Rebecca & Lola
BROOKLYN, NEW YORK

YOU TAUGHT YOUR DOG HOW TO BE A MAN...OR AT LEAST PEE LIKE A MAN.

This story isn't about gender norms or overcompensating male egos. It's about a dog learning to let go of a past love to eventually find peace in ways he never imagined.

My dog Donut loved squatting to pee. But when a male dog squats to urinate, the urine will inevitably make its way onto a front paw. Whether it's from splattering on the ground or just awkward angles, urine will unintentionally find its way onto appendages. One day, he was so misaligned that the yellow laser decided to skip right past the front legs altogether and go straight onto his chinny-chin-chin. When Donut realized what had occurred, he stirred into a chaotic frenzy of pure terror. How would he ever live this down? Would his mouth ever stop tasting like his own urine? After that, every time he urinated, with the PTSD of pee-mouth fresh in his mind he would panic-pinch and immediately begin looking for another suitable location to release the next one-sixteenth of his bladder.

The once somewhat innocent squat urination had been ruined forever.

And so I brought it upon myself, as his father, to teach him to pee like a man: to the side. When he would squat to pee, I would bend over and grab a hind leg and hold it up. He was extremely confused at first, panicking even more as the evacuation of his bladder became more and more convoluted.

But we kept at it, and after a year and a half of dogged persistence Donut finally began lifting his leg all on his own. A tiny doggy drumstick raising a rebellious paw toward the open skies—a glorious symbol of the triumph he's found trudging through the dark depths of urine-soaked depression. No longer will Donut live in fear, for he is a new man free of worry, anxiety, and precompletion pinching.

Marcus, Amy & Donut
BROOKLYN, NEW YORK 📷 DONUTMEISTER

YOU DO REALIZE WE HAVE A BACK YARD?

PEE (pë) v.
Like checking in online, peeing is like a dog's version of updating their Facebook status. It's a way of letting all the other pups in the neighborhood know where they've been, as well as a way to remind themselves of the bushes or fire hydrants that are worth revisiting.

YOU FELL IN LOVE WITH YOUR DOG AT FIRST SIGHT, SO MUCH SO THAT YOU ARRANGED TO HAVE HER DRIVEN TO THE UK FROM ROMANIA.

We had been looking for the right dog to rescue to complete our family and be a companion for our beagle, Mr. Budley, when my boyfriend stumbled across a site for Rolda, a Romanian dog rescue charity. That's when we saw Mia.

We learned that Romania suffers from a homeless dog epidemic, where more than sixty thousand dogs roam the streets of Bucharest alone. According to Rolda, thousands of strays are moved to public shelters, where they are housed in less than stellar conditions, and often are euthanized due to strict laws.

I browsed the rescue site and stumbled upon a picture of a skinny five-month-old puppy named Yamy. I knew she belonged with us, and called the charity's UK representative right away. After confirming that Yamy could be transported to the UK, and had received the appropriate vaccinations to qualify for a doggie passport, we arranged for a pet chauffeur company to bring her into the country.

Yamy made her big journey to us in October 2012. She was skin and bone, had scars everywhere and big patches of missing fur. We renamed her Mia and set about giving her all the love and care she deserved. She was scared of the stairs in our house, traveling in the car, as well as men and the big dogs we encountered on our walks. Slowly but surely, we managed to build up her trust in us and her surroundings.

Today, Mia's eyes sparkle with mischief and happiness. Mr. Budley showed her how to play and have fun. We still don't go away for holidays or weekend trips because we worry Mia wouldn't cope well in our absence. This is a small sacrifice to make, though. Mia is truly an angel in a doggie package and we spend every minute together. If I'm not with her, I feel like a bit of me is missing.

Sarah, Steve, Bud & Mia
DEVON, UNITED KINGDOM

CAN'T YOU JUST HANG YOUR HEAD OVER THE SIDE LIKE OTHER DOGS?

HUMAN BED

(hyü-men bed) n.

A heavenly place in which you become a blanket burrito and spend hours napping and farting while your hooman has to go out and work to support your lazy lifestyle.

THE CUTEST PUPPY SLEEPING POSITIONS THAT EVER EXISTED

**TONGUE OUT
SNOOZEDAY**

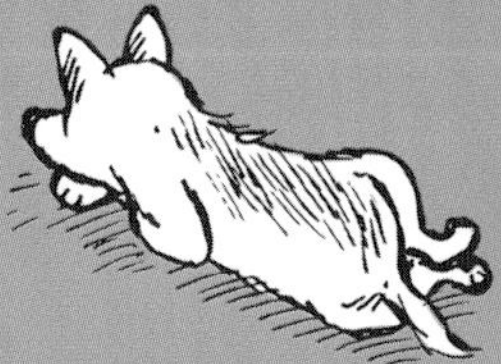

THE DESKTOP

THE BABUSHKA

**THE KANGAROO
POUCH**

**THE THING EVERY
DUDE HAS TRIED AT
LEAST ONCE**

**THE RABBIT
IN THE HAT**

**BITS TO
THE WIND**

**THE ACTUAL BALL
OF CUTENESS**

YOU BOUGHT A BIGGER BED SO YOUR DOG COULD HAVE "HALF."

My Australian Terrier, Judah Bear, used to sleep next to me on a full-sized mattress. It wasn't the best sleeping situation because he really likes to stretch out when he sleeps at night—horizontally, in the middle of the bed. I used to try to nudge him to the bottom of the bed, or switch him to a vertical position, but I always woke up on the edge of my bed while he'd be lounging across the center. I recently moved and decided it was the perfect opportunity to upgrade to a king-sized plush mattress. Now, when Judah Bear sleeps horizontally, I can just switch directions and sleep horizontally, too!

Casey & Judah Bear
BRONX, NEW YORK  CASEYANDJUDAHBEAR

YOU ARE YOUR DOGS' BED AND PILLOW.

Boogie and Marcelo love to sleep! There's only so much playing, eating, and hanging out they can do before the yawning and stretches kick in. Their best naps are always with each other, since they're best friends in real life and in dreamland. Although they're small (Marcelo is four pounds and Boogie is twenty-two pounds), they take up a whole lot of space. Marcelo likes to sprawl out on his back and Boogie loves to cuddle with heads, using my boyfriend and my foreheads as pillows. They're so snuggly, and always insist on touching either each other or a warm body at all times. Nighttime always involves grooming, Marcelo licking Boogie all over, and plenty of snoring.

Candy, Boogie & Marcelo
NEW YORK, NEW YORK 📷 BOOGIETHEPUG

YOU SLOW-DANCE YOUR DOG TO SLEEP EVERY NIGHT.

At just five months old, my dog, Finn, was found living on the street. He was so used to the wild that he had no idea how to sleep indoors. He fought bedtime by crying and hiding. As a last resort, I tried to calm him down by dancing. It has since become our nightly routine. We slowly sway around the living room as I sing him a tune—usually "Blue Moon" or "My Funny Valentine." It works like magic as he rests his head on my shoulder and drifts off to a peaceful sleep.

Rebecca & Finn
LOS ANGELES, CALIFORNIA ◯ FINNINLA

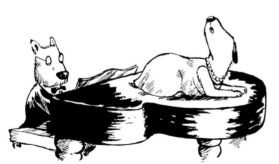

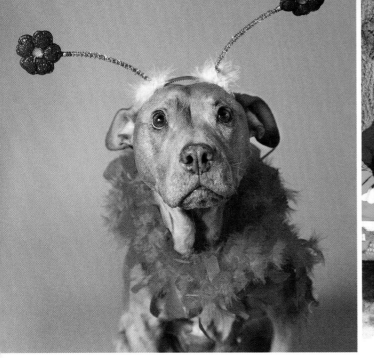

YOU CHAMPION A MOVEMENT TO SHOW THE WORLD YOU CAN'T JUDGE A DOG BY ITS PAST.

Handsome Dan was one of the dogs rescued from Michael Vick's Bad Newz Kennels. A lot of people wrote him off as a lost cause. No dog, they thought, could recover from such horrific abuse. But Dan's story is one of redemption. Today, Dan is not only happy—he is beloved. We can't imagine our family without him.

Tillie, our stylish diva, also had a rough start in life. Rescued from the second largest dogfighting investigation in U.S. history, Tillie became an ambassador for survivors of dogfighting. Before her passing in late 2015, she worked outreach events, lobbied at our state capitol to remove discriminatory language in dog-related legislation (and won!), and even had her own press

conference and coming-out party. Tillie's legacy serves as a reminder that a dog's future cannot be determined by her past. Long live #Team Tillie.

I started the nonprofit Handsome Dan's Rescue to focus on two specific groups of dogs; those who are unlikely candidates for adoption due to medical and/or behavioral issues, and survivors of dogfighting. Through Dan, Tillie, and other dogs who serve as symbols of hope, Handsome Dan's Rescue seeks to ensure equal treatment of all dogs, regardless of breed or background.

Heather, Handsome Dan & Tillie
CRANSTON, RHODE ISLAND
HANDSOMEDANSRESCUE.ORG

VICKTORY DOGS

In 2007, fifty-one American Pit Bull terriers were seized from NFL quarterback Michael Vick's dogfighting ring, where dogs suffered unimaginable abuse and often violent deaths. The term "Vicktory Dogs" refers to the twenty-two dogs rescued by Best Friends Animal Society. Although many believed that these dogs were mistreated beyond any chance of recovery, Best Friends Animal Society believed in giving them a chance.

Best Friends took in the Vicktory Dogs and began the challenging journey of giving them a new leash on life. These dogs suffered tremendous emotional trauma and needed sanctuary placement rather than being sent out to foster homes immediately. Although some of these dogs, including Dan, were fearful at first, after much care and time to recover, many have since settled happily into homes. Almost all of them have been adopted and are now living and loving alongside other dogs, families, and children—and even a cat!

The inspiring story of the Vicktory Dogs is a testament to the love that lives inside every dog, regardless of their breed or background. Even in the face of horrific circumstances, there is always hope.

YOU RISK DROPPING YOUR PHONE INTO WATER IF IT MEANS BEING ABLE TO DOCUMENT YOUR PUP'S LOVE FOR THE POOL.

I've accepted the fact that even though Jax is my best friend, water is his best friend. The pool may be sixty degrees, but since Jax lives for the water, I'll get in with him anyway.

Allison & Jax
PHOENIX, ARIZONA
JAX THE PUPPY

POOL (pül) n.

A giant water bowl that you can play in. It's so fun!

YOU CALL THE RESTAURANT TO LEARN ABOUT THEIR DOG-FRIENDLY SPECIALS FOR THE EVENING.

It doesn't always work, but sometimes it does.

Lara & Cookie
NEW YORK, NEW YORK 📷 PS.NY

Restaurant: Woofgang's
Star rating: ★★★★★
Reviewer: Cookie

The hoomans at Woofgang's will treat you like a king! I'm not exaggerating. When we arrived at our exclusive table on their gorgeous patio, the hostess didn't bring out just any old chair for me. No, no. Instead, she presented me with a tall thronelike thing of beauty. She called it a "High Chair"—one that was clearly fit for some kind of king or god. Everyone else had normal chairs, but this special one allowed me to look down on all the other patrons. It even had some Cheerios and pasta sauce shoved in the corners for me to happily lick up.

Throughout the meal, I was told what a good boy I was while enjoying several head scratches, and I was given plenty of treats by my servers/ servants. They even brought us biscotti at the end of the meal. (I wasn't allowed to eat it, but my hoomans thought it was a nice touch.) We will definitely be coming back.

YOU ARE SO MOVED BY YOUR DOG'S RESILIENT SPIRIT THAT YOU SHARE HIS HEALING POWER WITH OTHER HUMANS IN NEED.

Starting at a young age, Bocker modeled for brands and fashion magazines. He was featured on TV and in movies. I always knew I would do anything to make sure he had a good life. Then, in December 2014, he was diagnosed with lymphoma. Some people told me to "just let him go to his maker." I did everything in my power to heal him and alleviate his suffering, and he is now in remission. With more than 870,000 followers on Facebook, Bocker continues to raise awareness and support for those going through tough times to let them know that #NoOneFightsAlone. He is always ready to lend a helping paw through his therapy work and fund-raising for those less fortunate. Bocker continues to inspire the young and old—human and canines alike—with his generosity of spirit.

Marie & Bocker
MOUNT KISCO, NEW YORK BOCKER LABRADOODLE

YOU KNOW THAT YOUR DOG DOESN'T UNDERSTAND THE HOLIDAYS, BUT YOU DON'T UNDERSTAND THE HOLIDAYS WITHOUT HIM.

Every year I spend hours searching for the perfect gift for Rambo, and every year I realize that he enjoys playing with the wrapping paper much more than he enjoys playing with any of the actual gifts. So now I just buy one gift and rewrap it when he's not looking so he can unwrap it again and again and again. I hide the toy somewhere in the house and then we go on a hunt for it. After it's unwrapped and Rambo loses interest, I'll rewrap it and we'll play the game again. Funnily enough, my mom played the same trick on me when I was growing up!

Courtney & Rambo
PIEDMONT TRIAD, NORTH CAROLINA
📷 RAMBOTHEPUPPY

WRAPPING PAPER WRAPPED IN WRAPPING PAPER? YES!

CHRISTMAS (kris-mes) n.

That day when you are not only forced into a horrendously ugly sweater but are also supposed to just let some rando with a beard break into your house and steal a plate of cookies, and somehow not bark at him?!

LET ME GUESS: YOU WANT A BONE, TOO?

YOU TAKE YOUR DOG TO SIT ON SANTA'S LAP.

Convincing Santa to listen to the long list of toys and bones was ruff, but I wanted to make their first Christmas unforgettable.

Veronica, Jimmy, Bowser & Sadie
DAVIE, FLORIDA 📷 BOWSER_AND_SADIE

YOU DECORATE YOUR CHRISTMAS TREE WITH DOG TOYS.

It started out with just a few cute toys he had in his toy drawer. Then we thought, "Why not cover the entire thing and make it a dog toy–themed tree?" Our friends loved that we put a unique spin on traditional Christmas tree ornaments!

Katie & Chompers
SAN FRANCISCO, CALIFORNIA
CHOMPERSTHECORGI

YOU DON'T MIND THAT YOUR DOG GETS MORE GIFTS THAN YOU.

During a particularly tough day or an exceedingly late night at the office, I always remind myself that I work hard so my Bulldog can live a better life. While there were twelve presents with my name on them under our Christmas tree last year, little Miss Maya had 54. Totally normal.

Tania & Maya
LOS ANGELES, CALIFORNIA 📷 MAYA_ON_THE_MOVE

YOU GIVE YOUR DOG A HOMEMADE CHRISTMAS STOCKING.

My mother was never a dog person, but knowing how much Ollie means to us, she made an amazing effort to welcome him into her home. It was a great surprise to see Ollie's stocking hung with those of the rest of the family. What made it even more special was that Ollie's "grandmother" picked out the pattern, stitched it herself, and stuffed it full of treats and toys. Ollie had a very merry Christmas.

Liz & Ollie
LOS ANGELES, CALIFORNIA
📷 MROLLIEPANTS

YOU FORM THE MOST EXCLUSIVE OF PACKS THANKS TO YOUR HEALTHY OBSESSION WITH CORGIS.

Our love for Wally inspired us to form a Corgi meetup club called the FRAP Pack, a play on the term "Rat Pack." FRAP stands for Fun Random Acts of Play, a commonly used term in the Corgi community. We've held numerous park meetups, beach outings, and summer picnics. Our very first picnic saw over sixty Corgis in attendance!

We also plan our annual Corgsmas Pawty to celebrate the holidays in Corgi style—and to see tons of elf-dressed Corgi butts running in place. We hold

contests for Best Butt and Biggest Ears, play games of "Fido Says" and musical chairs, and, of course, dress up Wally as Santa Paws so the other pups can take pictures with him. Most important, Corgsmas also gives us the opportunity to give back by raising funds to help dogs in need!

Marc, Cynthia & Wally
WHARTON, NEW JERSEY 📷 WALLYTHEWELSHCORGI

YOU REFUSE TO TRAVEL BECAUSE YOU DON'T WANT TO LEAVE YOUR DOGS BEHIND.

Before becoming a part of our family, our pit bull/ Lab mix Theo was left at a veterinarian's office by his first family. If it hadn't been for my brother rescuing him, Theo wouldn't have made it to see his first birthday. We noticed that he suffered from severe separation anxiety, and it seemed to be strongest whenever my brother was missing.

One summer, my mom, my brother, and I went to Italy for several weeks while Theo stayed behind with my dad and Randy, our other pooch. During this time, Theo had trouble eating and began chewing on furniture, somehow managing to destroy one of the seat belts in my dad's truck! When we got back from our trip, he was unusually calm despite usually being super excited to see people. Instead of being his energetic and playful self, he just let my brother hug him for what seemed like forever. It was definitely a tearful moment for everyone!

My brother vowed that he wouldn't travel to any place unless the dogs would also be able to come, and he's kept his word. Our trips have mostly been to my grandparents' cottage, where there's plenty of room for Theo and Randy to run around!

Melissa, Randy & Theo
REPENTIGNY, QUEBEC ⓣ ACTUALDOGVINES

YOU HAVE GIVEN YOUR DOG A MILLION NICKNAMES AND THEY KNOW THEM ALL.

Lucy Goose, The Goose, Goosey, Baby Bear (when she's extra cuddly), The Vanilla Gorilla (when she does a muscular gorilla-like walk), Baby Beluga or Baby Pig (when she's looking a little pudgy), Frog Face or Frog Dog (she has frog legs and is quite the jumper!)

We actually say Lucy's nicknames more than her actual name. In fact, sometimes we don't even realize it when we have company over or if we're at the dog park, and it can be a little embarrassing to yell, "Come here, Goosey!" but most dog people understand. How can you not have a million nicknames when you've got a dog as cute as Lucy?

Laura, Andrew & Lucy
NEW YORK, NEW YORK
LITTLELUCYGOOSE

SIBLING

(sibliNG) n.

A pawtner in crime who you have
to share with your humans.

YOU TEACH YOUR KIDS THAT DOGS ARE FAMILY.

Sydney and Liberty aren't just dogs to Caleb and Cooper—they are their family. Today, when I asked Cooper, "Why do you love your dogs?" he looked at me and scoffed and said, "Mom, I love them because, well . . . because they are our family, duh!"

And that's just it. To these two little boys, their dogs are just as important as the air they breathe, the food they eat (and share), and the sports they play. They fight over which one can feed them in the morning while Mom and Dad are still in bed.

When Cooper, age four, found out that his dogs couldn't go on vacation with him, his emotional reaction was like nothing you could imagine: tears streaming down his face while hugging his dogs and crying hysterically, "But, I just love them so, so much!"

Lindsay, Sydney & Liberty
LAKE HAVASU CITY, ARIZONA
AUSSIE.POSSE

SEVEN REASONS DOGS ARE THE BEST SIBLINGS

1. **They are the only sibling who would never tell on you.**

2. **They never steal your clothes (besides a sock or two every now and then).**

3. **They are always there to listen after a long day.**

4. **They take the blame for any spilled milk or messes that you make. Farts too!**

5. **They don't care how bad a pitcher you are. They are just happy to play a game of fetch.**

6. **They clean up the food on your face instead of making fun of you for it.**

7. **They remind you not to worry without ever saying much.**

YOU FEEL YOUR HEART SWELL EVERY TIME YOU REALIZE YOUR DOG IS THE BEST BIG BROTHER YOUR KID COULD EVER HAVE.

Watching Carter grow up with Toby as his furry big brother has been incredible. My husband, Jake, and I always hoped that they would share a special bond, but the unconditional love they have for one another has far surpassed any of our greatest hopes or expectations. The greatest joy is watching as Carter experiences something for the first time (like preschool) and immediately runs home to tell Toby all about it. The same goes for Toby: when he gets a new toy he runs straight to Carter so they can share it together. I have no doubt that because Carter has the greatest furry big brother, he will always be a dog lover and continue to help rescue dogs like Toby.

Toby will soon be a big brother to another. Our Carter and Toby duo will soon be a trio!

Devin, Carter & Toby
INDIANAPOLIS, INDIANA 📷 CARTERANDTOBY

YOU ALWAYS GET A PRICKLE OF PRIDE WHEN YOU SEE YOUR DOG IN PROTECTOR MODE.

My wife and I recently added a new hooman member to the family, and Sakay, our Shiba Inu, has recently become her sworn protector! Whenever we have visitors over and they want to hang with Ari, Sakay immediately runs in front of her and blocks her off with a "You're gonna have to get through me first" expression. He does this every single time someone approaches Ari, so we actually ask our guest to stop in their tracks, bend down, and politely ask Sakay for permission to hold her. He sniffs, scoffs a bit, then looks at me for approval and trots away.

Sean & Sakay
COLUMBUS, OHIO 📷 SAKAYTHESHIBA

YOU LOVE THAT YOUR DOG IS YOUR DAUGHTER'S SIDEKICK.

Ziggy is a lot of things, but one of the things he is an expert at is being an awesome big brother. When Ziggy and our daughter Fiona wake up in the morning, they look for each other. They spend at least five minutes playing and cuddling before getting ready to conquer the day. When Fiona doesn't feel well or is crying, you will find Ziggy right there by her side. He's also very patient. Whether it's tight hugs or a little reading from sister, Ziggy sits patiently and plays along. We couldn't have been blessed with a better sibling for our baby girl!

Mayen & Ziggy
BOTHELL, WASHINGTON 🅞 ZIGGYTHEHAVANESE

YOU MADE A CUSTOM PILLOW OF YOUR DOG SO HE COULD BE AT THE HOSPITAL FOR YOUR DAUGHTER'S BIRTH.

When our daughter Jessica was getting ready to make her debut, we were so excited to welcome her into the world. The only problem was that her dog sibling Ernesto couldn't join the family at the hospital. Luckily, my husband's coworker had made an Ernesto pillow for us a few months earlier. The pillow joined other essentials in our "go bag" like clothes, toiletries, and our digital camera.

Although it may seem silly in retrospect, the pillow was really comforting when I went into labor. It was almost like Ernesto was there with us, welcoming his brand-new sister.

Jamie, Rob & Ernesto (Ernie)
BROOKLYN, NEW YORK

BABY (ba-be) n.
A tiny screaming human who shows up one day and steals your thunder and is somehow allowed to poop and scream in the house even though you are not allowed to.

YOU TEACH YOUR DOG TO ACTUALLY HELP WITH CHORES AROUND THE HOUSE.

I was loading the dishwasher one day when I dropped a dish on the floor. Jesse came running in, picked up the dish, and brought it to me. That was when I got the idea to teach him how to help out around the house. I taught him how to load the dishwasher by grabbing his dirty dish, putting it into the dishwasher, pushing the rack closed with his nose, and shutting the door with his paws. He picked up the tricks very quickly and would look at me with a happy smile on his face and an expression of, "What's next?!" He was so happy to learn something new, so we continued with fun "useful" tricks. I taught Jesse how to fetch the morning newspaper, help with the laundry, open and shut doors, go shopping, and much more. Now Jesse is my best chore helper. If he ever wanted to stop doing tricks we would stop, no questions asked, but his face lights up when he knows we are going to practice or learn tricks.

Heather & Jesse
LITCHFIELD PARK, ARIZONA 📷 JUSTJESSETHEJACK

YOU USE YOUR OVEN MOSTLY AS A PERSONAL HEATER FOR YOUR DOGS.

"My son pointed out that was crazy...."

I frequently turn both of our double ovens on to 400 degrees just for the dogs, so a nice warm draft blows down on their dog bed. They love sitting there and giving me "the look" to turn the ovens on if I haven't already. I don't really cook or bake much so it's a good use for the ovens, don't you think?

Angela, Myra, Doris, Lola & Frank
ROSEMOUNT, MINNESOTA ⊙ THREELITTLEFRENCHIES

YOU THINK YOUR DOG'S BREATH IS THE BEST THING YOU'VE EVER SMELLED.

Aria's excessive licking earned her the nickname "Mrs. Lickerston." She uses her kisses to calm me down after a stressful day, and she helps many others with her slobbering affection. Aria is a certified therapy dog and we volunteer at assisted-living homes, libraries, colleges, and hospitals. She's so sensitive to everyone's feelings and is always generous with her stinky kisses! It is therapy for me too, and I always leave with a full, warm heart.

Desiree & Aria
HOUSTON, TEXAS

THE BEST PART IS, FREE REFILLS!

YOU HAVE 14,978 PHOTOS OF YOUR DOG ON YOUR CELL PHONE, BUT THAT WON'T STOP YOU FROM BUYING TWENTY-FIVE HELIUM BALLOONS TO STAGE ONE MORE.

14,978. That's the number of pictures stored on my cell phone right now. Ninety-nine percent of those pictures are of Cooper and Fredrick. There are quite a few special occasions I try to capture of the boys, and Fredrick's first birthday was no exception.

I filled twenty-five balloons with helium, tied them, attached string, and arranged them in a wicker basket. Cooper and Fredrick had never seen so many balloons tied together and had a moment of panic! But once I pulled out the boiled chicken breast, the boys jumped in and out of the balloon-filled basket. I love my boys and will do anything to capture that one special moment (or fifteen thousand of them).

Esther, Cooper & Fredrick
MORTON GROVE, ILLINOIS
COOPER_THE_FRENCHIE

YOU CARRY YOUR DOG TO BED, FORTY POUNDS AND ALL, BECAUSE SHE'S AFRAID TO WALK TO BED BY HERSELF.

My dog, Izzy, has high anxiety. It often manifests itself as fear, and her greatest fear is the hallway that leads to her bed. When bedtime arrives, Izzy finds me and jumps on me to signal that she is ready to be carried to bed. She weighs forty pounds and carrying her is a workout, but if it helps to ease some of her anxiety, I'm all for it!

Jessica & Izzy
NEW BRAUNFELS, TEXAS 🖸 SITWAGHOWL

YOU REALIZE THAT YOUR DESIRE TO MAKE YOUR DOG HAPPY FORCED YOU TO DO THE SAME FOR YOURSELF.

The first time I saw Ziggy's face on Animal Haven's website, I started crying. He was staring straight into the camera and seemed to look right at me, knowing he would be my dog. On the day I picked him up, we were three steps out the door, and he suddenly wouldn't budge. Terrified, he pressed all thirty pounds of his weight into his oversized paws and refused to move. *I want to go back home,* he motioned with a jerk of his tiny head.

"Look." I beamed at him. "I know you don't know me, but I would never do anything to hurt you ever. We are going to be best friends. Will you trust me, Ziggy?" His spotted tail started beating against my leg, his boxy head broke into a smile, and he started to walk. It was almost three miles to his new home, but with every trash bag, bicyclist, and tourist stampede, Ziggy looked up at me for reassurance and bravely pranced and sniffed past each new obstacle. It's been like that for the past six years.

I've dealt with depression and anxiety my whole life and in the fall of 2014, after four wonderful years with Ziggy, I was at my lowest point ever. My desire to make my dog happy forced me to do the same for myself, so I applied to work at Bark & Co., knowing it would make me happy to make dogs happy. Despite my anxious jitters, Bark hired me. Ziggy and I walk almost three miles over the Manhattan bridge to and from work every day. Sometimes all it takes is a best friend to help you take the next step.

Zoe & Ziggy
BROOKLYN, NEW YORK

YOU TELL YOUR DOG THAT SHE'S THE BELLE OF THE BALL WITH THE AFTERBURP OF THE RED CARPET STILL ON HER BREATH.

This past year was our first time attending the Bulldog Beauty Contest, an annual event in Long Beach, California. From the moment we got there, Button was in cray-cray mode.

I tried my best to keep her under control, but as we lined up to walk the red carpet, I knew I was in trouble. She literally rolled down the red carpet and then tried to pull the carpet up and eat it, all while wearing a pink tutu—in front of the judges' table, no less.

Needless to say, she didn't place or win any ribbons that day, but she will always be a beauty queen to me: my crazy, bratty beauty queen.

Sierra & Button
REDONDO BEACH, CALIFORNIA
BUTTONTHEFRENCHIE

YOU PLAY HOOKY FROM WORK TO HAVE A PRETEND VACATION IN PRETEND-ANTIGUA WITH YOUR DOG.

I read somewhere that every few weeks the residents of Antigua bury each other up to their necks in sand and wriggle around. It serves as a natural full-body exfoliation. I have a family, a job, and a Bulldog, so it's hard to slip away to Antigua. Instead, I occasionally leave work early and take Sumo down to the beach—our happy place. We bury ourselves in the sand and wriggle around. We talk about coconut shrimp gumbo, cricket, and mojitos. We reminisce about the buccaneers who used to raid the island from their base in Tortuga. Sumo doesn't seem to care about the exfoliation, but he likes the cool wet sand on his skin and the conversation. Sometimes I feel like I don't know where he stops and I begin.

Beth & Sumo
VICTORIA, AUSTRALIA 📷 OPERATION_SUMO

HOW TO GET BEACH BODY READY (IF YOU'RE A DOG)

▶ When you hit the beach, you're gonna want to run around like a maniac chasing seagulls.

▶ Practice by chasing squirrels—the seagulls of the park! Work on your biceps by digging in dirt, or a child's sandbox.

▶ Prep for a nice doggypaddle in the ocean by splashing around in the toilet.

▶ Improve your fetch reaction time by snatching Frisbees from strangers in the park. The humans will enjoy the chase too!

▶ Get a head start on your tan by lying on the sunny part of the living room floor.

▶ Make sure your human trims your bikini line. We're talkin' full-on butt cut.

YOU GOT YOUR DOG A FITBARK.

My husband and I got Fitbits for ourselves around the summer of 2014. I had just learned that I was pregnant, and I wanted to make sure I was still active throughout. As we used our Fitbits, we found that both my husband and I were fairly competitive, and we also wanted to get Goosie involved. After some research, we found a dog activity tracker that we liked: the FitBark. Every night we check her steps, and if she hasn't reached her daily step goal, my husband, my daughter, and I run races from the living room to the front door and back again until she's gotten to her goal.

Alice & Goosie
NEW YORK, NEW YORK ◉ GOOSIERAHAEUSER

YOU LEARN HOW TO LOVE INDISCRIMINATELY FROM YOUR DOG.

It all began with my dog Biscuit who, once getting past his jealousy, fell in love with my two prairie dogs, Bing and Swarley. Then I got my ducks, and I was very careful in introducing them to the prairie dogs and Biscuit. Natural cuddlers, they all got along well and would snuggle up on my bed. I was never worried about the prairie dogs or Biscuit hurting the ducks because they've always been so delicate with little creatures. For this photo, I trained Biscuit to wait patiently while I put four small animals on his body.

Cassidy, Biscuit, Bing & Swarley
KINGWOOD, TEXAS ⊙ PRAIREDOGPACK

YOU BROUGHT YOUR DOG TO HIS FAVORITE WINDOW EVERY DAY WHILE HE HEALED FROM A CRIPPLING THIRTY-FIVE-FOOT FALL.

We were at a friend's place for a quick coffee on her condo's rooftop patio when Charlie, our French Bulldog, jumped onto a bench and over the patio fence. Before we could grab him, he ran to the edge of the roof and our hearts sank as he leaped and fell thirty-five feet to a concrete parking garage below. Just like that he disappeared. It didn't seem real.

Miraculously, he survived with two fractured shoulders and a jaw broken in three places. The veterinarian put three screws in Charlie's jaw, and even after having his front legs bound, he was determined to stand on his hind legs whenever he could.

We spent all summer hand-feeding him wet food. Despite being unable to walk for months, he stubbornly insisted on looking out the window or trying to go outside to stand in the grass. Each time, we lovingly carried him to the window or to the boulevard so that he could feel like a dog again. He would just stand there and look, watching people and dogs pass by, unable to move but still content and inspired to heal.

Today he's back to normal—running, jumping, playing, cuddling, and making us laugh. You wouldn't even know he fell but for a small scar on his chin.

Sandon & Charlie
CALGARY, ALBERTA 🔘 YOURDOGCHARLIE

YOU FOSTER A MILLION PUPPIES TO KEEP YOUR DOG HAPPY.

As naïve first-time foster parents, we imagined fostering would be like dogsitting for a friend. Little did we know it would completely change our lives. We agreed to care for two Aussie puppies, but when the transport arrived, there was a third puppy. After some research, the rescue discovered that a shelter volunteer had snuck Stella, the third puppy, into the van to give her a second chance. While the two Aussies were snuggly and shy, Stella the Stowaway was wild from the start, and I fell in love. Stella's foster companions were quickly adopted, but she loved having other pups in our family so much that we immediately agreed to two more. Every time a dog got adopted, Stella seemed lonely and we agreed to another playmate. Over her first year, Stella had nearly twenty foster siblings, ranging from four weeks to eight years old, who are now happily in forever homes all over the country.

Christina & Stella
BROOKLYN, NEW YORK ⬤ STELLADIGS

YOU HAVE A LIST OF THE BEST PLACES TO BUY BABY CLOTHES FOR YOUR DOG.

I started shopping at baby stores for my dog for several reasons. To begin, dog clothes are ridiculously expensive. Plus, most of the designs and buttons are on the back of the clothing, rather than the front. What's the point of having the cute details on the back if I'm taking pictures of my dog's furry little face from the front? Dog clothes also lacked variety with mainly jackets and shirts. Where else could I find adorable sweater vests, snuggly footie pajamas, and fedora hats?

A baby clothing store! Once I realized Rambo fit perfectly into baby clothes sized between three and six months, it was ON. Now, he has his own walk-in closet filled to the brim with button-down shirts, cardigans, and accessories.

Courtney & Rambo
PIEDMONT TRIAD, NORTH CAROLINA
⊙ RAMBOTHEPUPPY

TIPS FROM THE EXPERT: WHERE TO SHOP FOR YOUR DOG'S CLOTHES

CARTER'S
This is where I got Rambo's brown bear onesie, which is a favorite with his fans and followers. They have a lot of great sales (like half off!) around the major shopping holidays.

TARGET
Target has a great selection of onesies and seasonal hats. It's also worth noting that Rambo wears a nine-month-old onesie, even though his shirt size is smaller. Size up if you're going to buy your small dog a onesie.

KIDS' CONSIGNMENT STORES
Babies go through clothes incredibly fast, so you can find clothes that are like new (sometimes they ARE new) at baby/kids' consignment stores. I stick to the button-ups and sweaters, and steer clear of the onesies, since they're usually really worn.

BY COURTNEY, MOTHER OF RAMBO

YOU MAKE MISSING POSTERS FOR YOUR DOG'S FAVORITE TOY BECAUSE YOU CAN'T BEAR THE THOUGHT OF THEM BEING APART.

The first week Tuna came to live with me, my best friend gifted him a cute toy named Colin that I always referred to as a Hipster Alien. Tuna immediately fell in love with Colin and they were inseparable from the first day. A couple of years into their bromance, I accidentally left Colin at a park. Eek! I went back and searched everywhere for him, including a Dumpster*, but he was nowhere to be found.

*Yes, I literally jumped into a Dumpster for Tuna's toy!

Out of sheer panic, I tried to order Tuna a replacement Colin. I Googled "hipster alien doll named Colin" and discovered that Colin wasn't an alien at all, but an adorable creature from a company called Monster Factory. Although a replacement was on its way, I wasn't sure if Tuna would accept the new guy. So in a desperate final attempt to locate his favorite toy, I posted a "Missing Person" sign in the park, emphasizing that this was not a joke.

Two days later, I was contacted by a wonderful woman who explained to me that Bronze, her Golden Retriever, brought Colin back from the park. The following day we met up with Bronze's human to "retrieve" Colin, and she ended up inviting us to her private beach in Malibu—a vast contrast from the Dumpster.

Moral of the story: be relentless because both you and your dog win!

Courtney & Tuna
LOS ANGELES, CALIFORNIA ⊙TUNAMELTSMYHEART

HAVE YOU SEEN THIS GUY?

HE WAS LEFT AT THE PARK WEDNESDAY JUNE 19 AND HE IS MY DOG'S BEST FRIEND. HIS NAME IS COLIN.

IF YOU HAVE SEEN HIS WHEREABOUTS, PLEASE CONTACT COURTNEY AT C

THIS IS REALLY IMPORTANT.

THANK YOU SO MUCH!!!

PS. THIS IS NOT A JOKE ☺

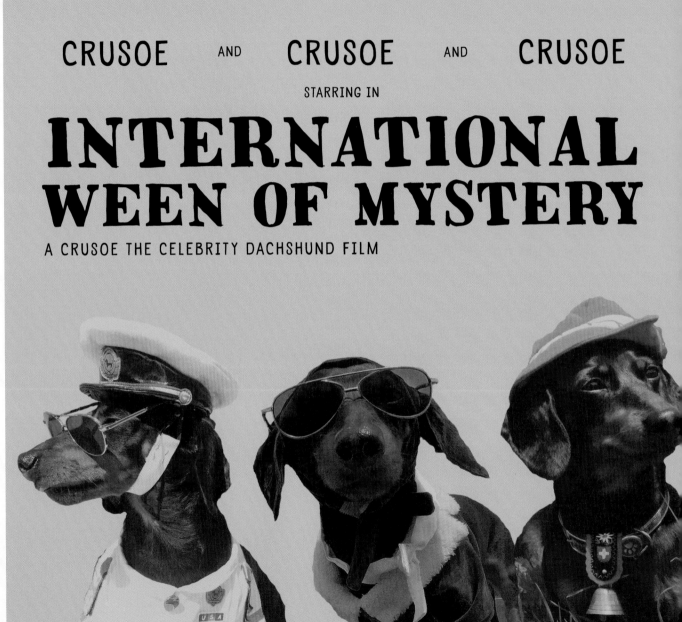

CRUSOE AND CRUSOE AND CRUSOE

STARRING IN

INTERNATIONAL WEEN OF MYSTERY

A CRUSOE THE CELEBRITY DACHSHUND FILM

"WHAT CAN I SAY? I JUST LOVE HIS RANGE. I'M CONVINCED HE KNOWS WHEN HE'S ACTING."
-RYAN, CRUSOE'S AGENT, MANAGER, DIRECTOR, PRODUCER, PPS (PERSONAL POOPER SCOOPER), AND DAD

ALSO STARRING
CRUSOE

AS **COP**

CRUSOE

AS **PRESIDENT**

AND INTRODUCING
CRUSOE

AS **HOUSEPLANT**

YOU CONSTRUCT ELABORATE NARRATIVES FOR YOUR DOG TO ACT OUT.

Crusoe is a little wiener dog of many talents, travels, and alter egos, and even boasts his very own *New York Times* bestselling book. His favorite activity in the world is fishing, but he also likes to prepare his own catch as Chef Crusoe. In his spare time he likes to fly planes, play street hockey with his brother, pull over speeders, hike up Swiss mountains, or pretend like he's working hard on the farm. When he's feeling ambitious, he runs for president, and when he's feeling lazy, he practices the motto that "Dachshunds need sunlight to grow."

Ryan & Crusoe the Celebrity Dachshund
OTTAWA, CANADA CRUSOE_DACHSHUND

YOU MAKE SPACE IN YOUR LIFE (AND YOUR BED) FOR ONE MORE SENIOR DOG.

I agreed to watch Gracie while her foster mom went out of town. My senior Cocker Spaniel had just passed away, so Gracie was my first foster in a while. She was around eleven years old and was such a gentle, quiet soul. I knew her age would make finding a forever home challenging, but with a big cross-border move in my future, adding her to the four pets we already had didn't seem right. After a week, while doing some gardening outside, I heard Gracie howling for me inside. In that moment, Gracie sounded exactly like my late dog. I was overcome with emotion; I knew that she was mine. I wanted her to know that she was loved and cherished in her golden years—her best years. She filled that gentle, wise void left by my old Cocker. She completes my home.

Holly, Gracie, Mini & Davey
OVERLAND PARK, KANSAS  PAWSOFOZ

In MY day, we ate dry kibble every day, and we LIKED it!

SENIOR DOG (se-nyer dog) n.

Like a fine wine, dogs simply get better with age.

YOU SPEND SO MUCH TIME ON YOUR DOG'S HEALTHY MEAL THAT YOU FORGET ABOUT YOUR OWN.

Johnnie always has a well-balanced diet with all organic protein and vegetables. My husband and I really try to eat healthy too, but sometimes we are so exhausted from spending an afternoon cooking all of Johnnie's meals for the whole month that we end up ordering pizza for ourselves while Johnnie eats his fancy organic veggies.

Larisse & Johnnie
RIO DE JANEIRO, BRAZIL 📷 JOHNNIE_THEFRENCHIE

BUTTHEAD
(but-hed) n.

A leader in the field of champions, a dog that refuses to play by any rules but their own. No matter how many times you dog-shame them, they will remain unabashedly proud of their work.

See also: hero.

SEVEN SUREFIRE SIGNS YOUR DOG IS A BONE-A-FIDE BUTTHEAD

You finally brought home the puppy of your dreams! The sun seems to shine brighter, the flowers seem to bloom earlier, and, of course, your home seems more like home. Nothing could be better. Then, suddenly you realize that underneath that cuddly appearance and those deliciously corn-chip-scented paws is an enormous buttface. A butthead that is now your baby–to be raised and cared for with all your heart. If you're unsure whether your pup is a buttface, check for these signs:

1. **There are a million toys strewn around the house, but your pup's toy of choice is underwear.** And glasses, slippers, hats, sweaters, necklaces, pajamas, keys, toilet paper...

2. **No matter the conditions, every walk turns into a forty-five-minute odyssey for the perfect patch upon which to make a urine offering.** To be fair, how would your dog know it was the absolute best patch without investigating every single one in the neighborhood, even in the dead of winter?

3. **Paying too much attention to your laptop? Time for your pup to lie down all over it!** Your e-mails look like "th1938x73lk[AW=-IS."

4. **Your pup has a legitimate addiction to things he shouldn't be eating.** "What fluff?? It wasn't me!"

5. **Your pup firmly believes "No!" means "Keep doing whatever you're doing repeatedly!"** "Want me to stop? COME AND MAKE ME!"

6. **When your pup wants attention, he goes immediately to his most hated behavior...like jumping into moving boxes you're trying to pack.** And scaling the counters when you're cooking, and chewing shoes when he feels like it, and stealing food always, and pretty much anything, as long as it's not sitting still.

7. **Your pup knowingly makes trouble, and when he does, he's staring directly at you...**and when your eyes meet, he knows he's won.

DONUT — RESIDENT BARK & CO OFFICE BUTTHEAD

YOU ACCEPT THAT YOUR DOG IS A TERRIBLE GARDENER, BUT YOU LOVE HIM ANYWAY.

Although our Golden Retriever had an entire backyard to play in, he decided to dig up our new potted plant instead. There goes our chance at a garden—and his fresh haircut.

Katherine & T-Bone
NEW CANAAN, CONNECTICUT
📷 GOLDENRETRIEVERS_

DIRT (dert) n.

A miracle compound that can clean your skin, nourish your hunger, and hide your valuables. Humans try to keep it out of the house because they're jealous of how much you love it.

YOU ACCEPT THAT YOUR DOG IS A FART MONSTER, BUT YOU LOVE HIM ANYWAY.

Frenchies are famous for their farts. Oscar isn't looking to dispel the rumor. He's the only creature who can steal a sincere smile from our faces whenever he farts in bed while we're watching a movie. And the funny part is that he turns around and looks at us as though we did it!

Andre & Oscar
ASTORIA, NEW YORK ◉ OSCARFRENCHIENYC

YOU ACCEPT THAT YOUR DOG IS A SANDWICH THIEF, BUT YOU LOVE HER ANYWAY.

Andi is a thief. She has stolen hundreds of thousands of meals from dogs and people. Great is her gaze with greed.

Lisa & Andromeda (Andi)
BROOKLYN, NEW YORK 	WEIRDWIENER

OH, YOU MEAN YOU DIDN'T WANT ME TO POOP ON THIS RUG?

NO! (no) adv.

Keep doing exactly what you're doing.

YOU ACCEPT THAT YOUR DOG IS PRETTY MUCH ALWAYS COVERED IN MUD, BUT YOU LOVE HIM ANYWAY.

It is a very good thing Marlo is brown, as more times than not he is covered in some kind of mud. He loves swimming in murky water, running through pluff mud, and rolling around in anything stinky. I have traded in my white sheets, pristine floors, and clean car windows for the best dog I could ever have.

Gabrielle & Marlo
CHARLESTON, SOUTH CAROLINA 📷 TUCKER_MARLO

I COULDN'T REACH THE TOWELS.

MUD (muhd) n.
A refreshing body wash available at a fabulous array of outdoor locations.

YOU ACCEPT THAT YOUR DOGS DECIDE TO "REDECORATE" YOUR HOME, BUT YOU LOVE THEM ANYWAY.

When my two Huskies came into my life it was an unexpected blessing in disguise.

Theo took it upon himself to eat my couch and left its remains scattered around the house. After the couch was gone, he moved on to the carpet, the TV stand, and finally the TV. In the course of a hundred days, my home was transformed into an empty Mondo art gallery scattered with dog toys. Then his littermate ended up homeless, and it was love at first sight for us. We quickly discovered that her favorite lounging spot was on the kitchen counters, and her favorite pastime activity was emptying out the cabinets and pulling apart the stove. So, of course, we puppyproofed the kitchen with cabinet locks, removed the burners, and put the countertop equipment on top of the cabinets.

Denise, Theo & Desna
AUSTIN, TEXAS KNEE_DEEP_IN_FUR

YOU ACCEPT THAT YOUR DOG SUFFERS FROM SERIOUS MONDAY MORNING SYNDROME, BUT YOU LOVE HIM ANYWAY.

Every Monday I wake up to Bruno's stinkeye. He usually grumbles when the alarm goes off and refuses to get out of *my* bed. If it's raining on a Monday, he also refuses to do his business, and if it's a really *bad* Monday, he won't even eat his breakfast. I love him because he is totally on my Monday-morning level.

Lindsay & Bruno
LONDON, UNITED KINGDOM
 BRUNOTHEMINIDACHSHUND

UGH, MORNINGS...

COFFEE

BUTTHEAD DOG PEOPLE PROBLEMS

💩 When you're kissing your dog and they sneeze... in your mouth.

💩 When you get them a new toy but your dog prefers your shoes or your underwear.

💩 When your dog finds a piece of poop that's not theirs and says to themselves, "You know what? I should eat that."

💩 When you're trying to have a conversation on the phone and your dog decides it's the perfect time to relentlessly squeak their loudest toy or bark at some nonexistent squirrels.

💩 When you're trying to open a poop bag with no discernible opening.

💩 When people tell you how to be a pup parent.

💩 When your dog licks their butt...then licks your face.

💩 When you're trying to take the perfect photo and they keep looking away.

💩 When your dog scoots their butt on the carpet.

💩 When your dog sniffs your guests' crotches when you invite them over.

💩 When your dog digs through the trash and eats things they most definitely should not be eating. Specifically tampons.

YOU ACCEPT THAT YOUR DOG EXPECTS YOU TO SPEAK DOG, BUT YOU LOVE HIM ANYWAY.

I don't *ever* question my dog's logic. I decided to give him a bath outside and when he immediately proceeded to dry himself off in the mud, who was I to say no?

Amber & Bear
FORT COLLINS, COLORADO 📷 CLASSYASPUP

YOU ACCEPT THAT YOUR DOG HAS LETHAL FARTS, BUT YOU LOVE HER ANYWAY.

Dear Ruby,

Your farts. They're toxic. Day in and day out you prove that my gag reflex is alive and well. When I'm with you, I wish I didn't have a sense of smell. I have to wonder if there is something wrong with your sense of smell. Or maybe you just like the smell of your own farts. What I'm sure of is that you don't give a darn. And I love you for that.

Love,

Kaitlin, Your Mom

Kaitlin & Ruby
BROOKLYN, NEW YORK

YOU ACCEPT THAT YOUR DOG IS A MASTER MANIPULATOR, BUT YOU LOVE HIM ANYWAY.

When I visited the shelter, my intention was to just ask some questions about potentially adopting a dog in the future. The *few-months-away* future. I opened my car door as I was leaving only to have a small dog jump into the driver's seat and give me the saddest puppy-dog eyes. He had broken out of his crate, snuck out, and followed right behind me to the car. Buddy came home with me that day.

As it turns out, he breaks out of crates a lot. Seven of them to date, and I've since given up on getting any more. He also sneaks out of doors a lot, and only comes back for the promise of treats. He knows how to work a crowd, and anytime he feels in need of a snack, or cuddles, or (most often) forgiveness for the latest trouble, he directs his sad face to everyone present until he gets his way. And it works every time. We've had a great two years together, with many more to come.

Kelsy & Buddy
WORCESTER, MASSACHUSSETTS [○] BUDDYTHEJERK

YOU ACCEPT THAT YOUR DOGS FEAST ON CAT POOP, BUT YOU LOVE THEM ANYWAY.

My two dogs, Treyis and Wallie, are usually well behaved...unless there is cat poop involved.

Every time I let them out to potty, they run as fast as their little legs can take them to their favorite dinner spots in the yard and gorge themselves on cat doo-doo. So one day, I decided to spray the cat poop with hot sauce. When I finished up the yard and let the dogs out, they bolted to their favorite spots and proceeded to chow down as if they were invited to Thanksgiving dinner. They ate the poop with such enthusiasm that it almost felt like they were attempting to insult me by indulging in my special recipe of fire-blended cat turds.

The next morning, Treyis had gas that can't even be explained. I literally had to look around to see if he had laid a pile somewhere. All I can hope for now is that the cats dislike the smell of hot sauce and quit using the yard.

Leah, Treyis & Wallie
MILLS, WYOMING
WARNERHASMUK

FOLLOW YOUR BLISS...AND THEN ROLL IN THAT $&*%

PAWTY ANIMAL (paw-tee a-ne-mel) n.

When you overdo it on the treats and puke in the corner so that no one notices...then eat that puke...and then go back for more.

My Old English Sheepdog Rudie, aka Rude Dog, learned how to open the fridge randomly a few years after he was adopted. From then on, he would periodically open it, take out a few things, and snack on them while I was gone. I decided to try duct-taping the fridge shut, but he soon learned how to peel the duct tape off. I tried a childproof fridge lock. He started dragging the fridge across the kitchen. Terrified it would tip, I anchored it to the wall. He ripped it out of the drywall the next day and then broke the lock off. The fridge is now padlocked shut and I had a custom gate built so that he cannot enter the kitchen. His reign of fridge terrorism has come to an end.

Heather & Rudie
CHICAGO, ILLINOIS ⬤ RUDIELOVESTRASH

YOU ACCEPT THAT YOUR DOG IS A HOUSEHOLD TERRORIST, BUT YOU LOVE HIM ANYWAY.

EVERYTHING RUDIE HAS EATEN

- blender
- 5 salad plates
- 2 dinner plates
- pie stand
- 1 stove
- 1 fridge
- 1 leftover
  pizza in the fridge
- 2 tomatoes
- a brick of cheese
- a package of tortillas
- 1 screen window
- 3 sets of blinds
- 1 grooming table
- 3 potted plants
- many trashes

HOW TO WINTERIZE YOUR DOG

❋ They may look silly but a sweater or coat is the easiest way to keep your pup warm when the temperature drops.

❋ If there's any chance a hard rain's gonna fall, be sure your dog is as amphibious as possible in a water-repellent raincoat.

❋ Snow and salt can be a cruel combo when it comes to your pup's paws. Protect them with galoshes or rubber booties—and be sure to clean and dry their paws immediately after your walk.

❋ Your dog's body is working overtime trying to keep warm, so it's a good idea to supplement their diet with extra treats and always make sure they stay hydrated.

❋ Protect and soothe noses, paws, and ears with healing balms formulated specifically for dogs.

❋ Limit time outdoors and make sure your pup has a comfortable nook where they can warm up once they're back inside.

YOU KEEP YOUR DOG'S FAVORITE PATCH OF GRASS SNOW-FREE ALL WINTER SO THEIR PAWS DON'T GET COLD.

Wisconsin winters can be brutal, so we made sure Zappa's feet never had to touch the snow by diligently shoveling her favorite patch of grass all winter long.

Sadie, Rosalie & Zappa
PEWAUKEE, WISCONSIN 📷 THE_REAL_ZAPPA

YOU BUILD YOUR DOG A FAKE GROUNDHOG HOLE TO MAKE SURE HE STAYS SAFE FROM MURDEROUS VARMINTS.

My Dachshund Ammo has a super strong hunting instinct, so spending a lot of his time on our family's twenty-acre horse farm is a dream for him. Since Dachshunds were originally bred to go down holes to hunt badgers, Ammo tends to push the boundaries on the farm in search of all of the groundhog holes he can find. I've pulled him out by his tail too many times to count, and even had to dig him out from underground on some occasions!

Being an overprotective dog mom, I always worry he's down some hole having a vicious fight with a groundhog. To ease my worry, I started having him wear a GPS pet tracker, I filled in all the holes around the farm that I could find, and I even make him wear an LED glow collar at night so he's more visible. Despite my efforts, he began wandering farther from the farm in search of his next hunting hole, so I got a little more creative. I ordered a bottle of rabbit scent off the Internet and set out to dig him a hole much closer to the barn. Using a post hole digger, I made a fake hole (with two entrances because groundhogs have a front and back door) and used a spray bottle to cover the area with rabbit scent. Ammo goes crazy for the animal scent trailing around the areas and digs at the hole for hours. Every day we are out on the farm I re-spray the hole to keep him close and out of danger. He's happy he has a hole, and I'm happy I don't have to dig my dog out from underground anymore. We both sleep better at night!

Kyley & Ammo
DOWNINGTOWN, PENNSYLVANIA
AMMOTHEDACHSHUND.COM

YOU GIVE YOUR DOG THE KEYS TO NYC AND TELL HIM HE'S THE MAYOR.

When Hamilton Pug ventures out into his city (sometimes alternatively referred to as "New York City"), it is not uncommon for fans to recognize him and for future friends to stop and say hello. It would be an understatement to say that Hamilton has mastered the art of the meet and greet. In fact, some people call him "The Mayor." It's a fitting title, so we let him believe that he's in charge. His brother Rufus is his bodyguard.

Wendy, Steve, Hamilton & Rufus
NEW YORK, NEW YORK ◉ HAMILTONPUG

YOU SQUEEZE-HUG YOUR DOG JUST A LITTLE TOO TIGHTLY SO YOU CAN HEAR THAT ADORABLE OLD MAN NOISE THAT HE MAKES.

I feel like as he has gotten older he is more vocal and loves to be hugged extra tight for hours. He's always the little spoon.

Kacee & Diesel Todd
NORTHLAKE, TEXAS 🔘 DIESEL TODD

YOU TREAT YOUR DOG LIKE SHE'S A MOVIE STAR AND GIVE HER THE A-LISTER TREATMENT.

Toast loves going to the spa. She loves her robe and her facials, and she loves taking a nap and tuning out the world. We take her down to Palm Beach to the Brazilian Court Hotel, where they have an entire menu of doggie facials. In the city, we head up to the Surrey for a full menu of dog delights served on silver platters.

And why do I give her the A-lister treatment? Because she's actually an A-lister.

Katie & Toast
NEW YORK, NEW YORK
⬛ TOASTMEETSWORLD

THINGS YOU CAN SAY TO YOUR DOG, BUT NOT ANOTHER HUMAN

Note: all of these things technically can be said to a human. However, we strongly recommend you refrain from doing so.

✘ "Who's a cutie? Do you want to sit on my lap?"

✘ "If you go poop I promise to rub your belly for at least twenty minutes."

✘ "I love that your tongue is too big for your mouth!"

✘ "Your jowls are so luxurious! I want to bask in their glory forever!"

✘ "After I bathe you I'll put you on your leash and take you for a walk."

✘ "I'll give you a treat if you don't pee on the doctor this time."

✘ "I'm having your testicles removed for your own good."

✘ "Thanks for eating that spider the other day. I'm still kind of grossed out, but thanks."

✘ "You're so old! And adorable! Can I pick you up?"

✘ "How do you like your new crate?"

YOU OFTEN FIND YOURSELF HAVING CONVERSATIONS WITH OTHER HUMANS USING YOUR "DOG VOICE" AND YOU DON'T EVEN REALIZE IT.

I am so crazy about my dog that I have basically personified her by giving her a human "Gizzy voice." Sometimes I find myself having conversations with other humans using only this voice, which is entirely from her perspective. "Gizzy voice" is best used in awkward moments to help cut tension and bring a bit of humor to a stressful situation. Telling your best gal pal her new boyfriend sucks isn't always the easiest thing to do, but Gizzy has no problem keeping it real and bringing truth to any situation.

Lisa & Gizmo
NEW YORK, NEW YORK 📷 NEWYORKDOG

YOU KNOW THAT YOUR MORNING IS NOT COMPLETE WITHOUT A FRENCHIE MOON AND THE RISING SUN.

When I wake up, I'm always guaranteed to find a bum or snort in my face.

Candy, Sumo, Ayumi, Tonka & Mochi
LEHIGH VALLEY, PENNSYLVANIA
3BULLDOGGES

ARSESTROLOGY

YOU KNOW THAT YOUR DOG SAVED YOUR LIFE IN SO MANY MAGICAL WAYS.

Every day I write about dogs that capture my heart, but no dog has ever filled my life with as much joy as my own Shiba Inu, Buttons. I adopted Buttons from NYC Shiba Inu Rescue. He was rescued from a hoarding situation and was terrified of everything. Anything new, including me, scared him. After a lot of tears, patience, and consistent training, we started to trust each other. Then he started to trust the world—and then he started to help me trust the world.

I'm legally blind. Before I got Buttons, I struggled with stairs and collided into people and things constantly. Buttons noticed and, all on his own, started taking his steps one at a time, ensuring I could follow his path. He began to lean into me if there was an object that I was in danger of hitting. For a year, Buttons and I worked on our training so he could become my service dog. We're truly a team; I have to listen to him as much as he has to listen to me.

The first time we went to a store together, I cried when we got home. I had no idea how much independence I had lost until he gave it back to me. With him at my side, I'm not afraid or anxious that when I go out in public I'll hurt myself or someone else by walking into them.

Buttons is incredibly dedicated, and his primary focus is making sure I'm safe, both physically and emotionally. In the last few years, I've lost two family members. In my devastation, it was Buttons who grounded me, dragging me back to reality when I so desperately needed it. There are no words to capture just how much I love him.

Regina & Buttons
NEW YORK, NEW YORK

YOU MAKE YOUR DOG COOKIES WITH HIS NAME EMBOSSED.

I started baking homemade cookies for my dog Oliver because I thought he had food allergies. When it turned out that he didn't have allergies, I kept baking. By that point, Oliver and his friends at the dog run loved them too much to stop! I also perfected my recipe, discovering that peanut butter and pumpkin are essential ingredients. Last year, to up my cookie game, I ordered a cookie cutter embossed with his name.

Martha & Oliver
NEW YORK, NEW YORK 📷 MGOLD212

THE PAWFECT DOG COOKIE

INGREDIENTS

- ½ cup peanut butter
- 1 cup pure pumpkin purée
- 1 egg
- 1¾ cups whole-wheat flour (can use rice flour if your dog has wheat sensitivities)
- 1 teaspoon baking soda
  Optional:
- 1 teaspoon dry milk

DIRECTIONS

1. Preheat the oven to 350 degrees F.
2. Mix all ingredients together.
3. Roll out the dough on a well-floured surface to about ¼-inch thick.
4. Cut with your favorite cookie cutters.
5. Bake on a cookie sheet for 15–20 minutes, then rotate the pan and bake another 15–20 minutes.
6. Cool completely and store in an airtight container.

YOU BLOW YOUR ENTERTAINMENT BUDGET ON A FOURTH OF JULY SHOW THAT YOUR PUPS WILL SLEEP THROUGH.

This past Fourth of July, we spent the day grilling everything and lighting sparklers, which Henry and Penny couldn't take their eyes off. It seems our pups had eaten too many hot dogs and hamburgers that day because when the fireworks began (and they were LOUD), we found them both passed out on the floor and impossible to wake!

Sarah, Henry & Penny
PITTSBURGH, PENNSYLVANIA
⊙ HENRYANDPENNY

YOU ORGANIZE PUG POOL PARTIES OF EPIC PROPORTIONS.

When Giles was just six months old, he started to have Pug playdates with friends he made on Instagram. We discovered they all loved swimming, so we've been hosting Pug pool parties ever since. Giles can sense the pawty buzz on the day of as he waits for his friends to arrive. We have all the pups dress up for dinner—and then everyone goes home and sleeps for two days straight.

Deborah, Angel, Isabelle & Giles
BLOOMFIELD, NEW JERSEY 🔘 GILESTHEPUG

PAWTY (paw-tee) n.
When you get peanut butter–wasted and you wake up without your pants on, but then you're like "Why was I wearing pants, I'm a dog..."

YOU DON'T MIND THAT YOUR DOG GETS MORE MAIL THAN ANYONE IN THE HOUSE.

Darla usually gets four or five packages a month (thanks to her Instagram popularity!) and she opens most of them. She gets all kinds of things in the mail: dog food, treats, collars to model, prizes from a contest, and of course her lovely BarkBox! She thinks every package that lands at our door is hers. She scares the mailman by trying to grab the box if he attempts to deliver to our door and has also run up to him many times to inspect his bag.

Andrea & Darla
HAMPTON, NEW BRUNSWICK 📷 DARLADAISY_

YOU PUT YOUR DOG IN SCHOOL JUST SO YOU CAN HAVE THE GRADUATION PHOTOS.

Since Penelope was my first puppy, I simply *had* to enroll her in puppy class. After six long weeks of learning how to sit and stay, graduation day finally arrived! She demonstrated her tricks flawlessly and passed with flying colors. The only thing better than her outstanding performance was when she surprised everyone with her love for the graduation cap. Funnily enough, I didn't buy my own college graduation pictures, but I had to have copies of hers!

Deanna & Penelope
WANTAGH, NEW YORK 📷 P.THE.FRENCHIE

YOU FREQUENTLY ROLE-PLAY TO EASE YOUR DOG'S SEPARATION ANXIETY.

Before I adopted Dingo, I fostered him for a test drive. He had intense separation anxiety and couldn't be left alone in the apartment for more than a few seconds before scratching at the door and letting out the saddest whimper of defeat I've ever heard. So I Googled "antidotes for separation anxiety."

I read an article about practicing separation anxiety exercises that indicate to your pup that you're leaving (putting on your coat, lacing up your shoes, jingling your keys) and then just staying in the apartment instead of leaving. So there I found myself one particularly warm evening in the fall wearing my winter gear, sitting on the couch and saying things like "See? Here I am!" Once Dingo was calm, I would move toward the entrance, decked out from head to toe in winter garb, and leave the apartment for twenty seconds at a time before reentering with an emphatic "GOOD BOY, DINGO!" (as the article suggested). I did this about two hundred times over the course of the weekend, and even though my neighbors who passed this heavily winter-geared dude in the middle of an Indian summer never looked at me the same, it was all worth it. I adopted Dingo a week later and now I get separation anxiety when I leave him.

Daniel & Dingo
BROOKLYN, NEW YORK

YOU ALWAYS GIVE YOUR DOGS FIRST PICK OF THE BED.

My dogs, Riley and Killer, are best friends and do almost everything together. This includes snuggling up like two perfect little fur burritos in the middle of my bed before I have a chance to save myself a spot.

Do I move them? Are they being super rude? Should I bribe them out with a treat? Of course not, because I am a dog person.

Alicia, Riley & Killer
LOS ANGELES, CALIFORNIA 📷 MORILEYMOPROBLEMS

THE TOP 5 DESTINATIONS FOR DOG LOVERS

1. THE MOM-AND-POP STORE THAT GREETS YOUR DOG WITH FREE TREATS.
What's not to love about them? They know their pupstomer and really go above and beyond, so...

2. THAT ONE CAFÉ THAT ALLOWS DOGS INSIDE.
You can spend countless hours here just chilling with your pup and a cup of yummy coffee.

3. THE LOCAL DOG PARK.
It's been rated as the neighborhood's hottest go-to spot for dog lovers with dogs, dog lovers without dogs, and dog lovers looking to meet other dog lovers.

4. THE BIG TREE AROUND THE CORNER FROM YOUR HOME.
It's where all the pups pee and where your dog gets their social pupdates from.

5. YOUR BED.
Every dog lover knows that the **#1 Destination** is their bed because NOTHING trumps cuddling your dog all weekend long.

WHEN YOU TOLD ME HE COULD DOGGIE PADDLE...

YOU ALMOST ALWAYS PLAN WEEKENDS AROUND WHETHER YOUR DOG IS ABLE TO COME ALONG.

My boyfriend, Kurt, and I take Lily everywhere with us as she's more than just family. This past summer, Kurt erected a Lily pad on the front of his kayak for her to ride on. It took her a few trips before she had the courage to venture out onto it, but by Labor Day, she was doing her balancing act and had taken over as captain of the ship.

Sarah, Kurt, Porter & Lily
HOLLISTER, CALIFORNIA ⊙ LITTLELILYANDPORTER

YOU ENTERED A CUTE PHOTO CONTEST WITH A PICTURE OF YOUR DOG POOPING.

We entered Bane into a cute picture contest when he was a pup. Other entries were of dogs doing normal things like playing in the park. We choose a picture of Bane potty training and pooping on his wee pad. The grand prize was for a thirty-by-thirty-inch oil painting of the submitted picture. Now we have a painting of Bane pooping hanging across from the toilet in our bathroom.

Cassie, Mike & Bane
NEW YORK, NEW YORK ◉ BANETHEBULLDOG

YOU AND YOUR SIBLINGS LIVE THREE HUNDRED MILES APART AND ONLY STARTED HAVING REGULAR VISITS SO THAT YOUR DOGS CAN PLAY TOGETHER.

My sister and I have lived far away from one another for the last fifteen years, but we only recently started visiting each other regularly so that our dogs can play together. My Puerto Rican pup, Luna, and my sister's Sudanese Hound, Bramble, are best friends. Watching them tear around the yard together, team up to stalk squirrels, and snuggle up against each other to nap is worth all the frequent-flyer miles and traffic jams in the world. And it's made me and my sister, who were already close, even tighter. We love our pups so much that we even had a cake made with both of them rendered in frosting for our brother's birthday. He doesn't have a dog yet, but as soon as he does, he can join our club!

Gigi & Luna
NEW YORK, NEW YORK

YOU WILL HAPPILY TAKE YOUR MEAL À LA BLAND SO YOU CAN USE THE LAST OF YOUR EXTRA VIRGIN OLIVE OIL FOR YOUR DOG'S MEAL.

My mini dachshund Chutney is a fussy eater. I tried changing her food. I tried feeding her biscuit after biscuit, one at a time. I even tried mixing people food in with her kibble, but nothing would work. One day, at my wits' end, I tried drizzling some olive oil onto her plate and she licked it clean within seconds. Now Queen Chutney gets the fanciest olive oil I can afford while I use the supermarket-brand vegetable oil to cook with!

Hannah, Chutney & Branston
CHANDLER'S FORD, UNITED KINGDOM
CHUTNEY_MUTTNEY

YOU MAKE SURE TO LEAVE YOUR DOGS' THEIR FAVORITE SPOTIFY PLAYLIST OR YOUTUBE VIDEO ON LOOP WHENEVER YOU LEAVE THE HOUSE.

Every day before we leave for work, we make sure to leave the TV on or have music playing so the pups don't get anxious or lonely while we are away.

Notable YouTube clips include Drunk Squirrels, Squirrels Gone Wild, and Puppies vs. Tennis Balls.

Allen, Lora, Fugee & Starla
VALENCIA, CALIFORNIA
 THEFUGEE

A DOG'S GUIDE FOR WHEN A HUMAN IS OUT OF THE HOUSE

RULE #1
Protect the house against squirrels at all costs (to the neighbors' sanity).

RULE #2
Keep the toilet water levels nice and low.

RULE #3
Turn the laundry pile into your own enchanted play castle.

RULE #4
Bark at all the crazy people on daytime TV.

RULE #5
Practice opening the kitchen cabinets to prepare for the Great Treat Heist...

RULE #6
Finally catch that no-good vacuum cleaner while he's sleeping.

RULE #7
Poker with the guys.

RULE #8
Practice happy dance moves to showcase when your person returns.

RULE #9
Definitely don't clean.

YOU ADOPTED A DOG TO BE YOUR DOG'S PARTNER IN CRIME.

A little over two years ago, Peabody developed a rare blood disease and almost died. For months, we slept on the kitchen floor next to him in case he needed anything during the night. He responded to the treatment, and after he'd been on multiple medications for a year, we were able to wean him off them completely. Now that he was healthy and energetic again, we thought he might be lonely during the workday, so we decided it was time to bring home a puppy. We weren't sure how Peabody would react to Mr. Neville, but his loving response exceeded all our expectations. He became a model big brother. They sleep side by side and are generally inseparable.

Roberta, Peabody & Mr. Neville
HOBOKEN, NEW JERSEY

YOU TURN YOUR NYC APARTMENT INTO A PHOTO STUDIO FOR YOUR DOG.

Chloe has a magical ability to make anyone smile. Aiming to spread happiness, I created an Instagram account to share her with the world. Now she's become an Instagram star, and converting my tiny apartment into a photo studio every now and then is just part of how the magic happens.

Loni & Chloe
NEW YORK, NEW YORK ⊙ CHLOETHEMINIFRENCHIE

YOU KNOW THAT YOUR DOGS ARE THE REASON YOU GET OUT OF BED EACH MORNING.

My dogs are my world. When I am having a bad day or an anxiety attack, Leonard sits on me and cuddles me until I feel better. Any time I start to cry or freak out, he is there. Penny is my heart dog. Billie Jean came into my life unexpectedly, and she has been a blessing ever since, and continues to be feisty and full of spunk. I have had my sweet Gizzy for almost six years now. She's full of attitude and her age doesn't seem to be showing any signs of slowing her down anytime soon. These four dogs help me wake up every day and put me at ease when I sleep at night. They are the reason I am still here.

Heather, Penny, Leonard, Billie Jean & Gizzy
MOUNTAIN HOME, IDAHO 📷 PENNYANDLEONARD

YOU TURNED YOUR HOME INTO A MICROBREWERY JUST TO PUT YOUR DOG ON THE LABEL.

We had the opportunity to brew our own beer and were most excited about incorporating our dog's name into the beer's name. When I heard we were going to brew the beer at a facility, the first thing I did was think about how Nacho would look on the label and what type of catchy name I could come up with. We decided on a name pretty easily because what describes a Bulldog better than "burly," especially when you're naming a Belgian beer? We brewed a keg's worth and when I posted a picture of it on Instagram, I got a handful of e-mails asking when it would be in stores and how to purchase it. Unfortunately, I had to tell them it was a limited edition—just for his humans.

Jenna & Nacho
BOSTON, MASSACHUSETTS 📷 NACHODOGG

A GUIDE TO BREWING NACHO'S "BURLEY BELGIAN ALE"

TAILS UP!

STEP ONE

COME UP WITH A NAME INVOLVING NACHO

STEP TWO

TAKE PICTURES OF NACHO

STEP THREE

MAKE 1,000 NACHO LABELS

STEP FOUR

BREW BEER (WHATEVER THAT MEANS)

YOU ATTACH A BASKET TO YOUR BIKE SO YOU CAN BRING YOUR DOG WITH YOU EVERYWHERE.

Bunny is heartbroken when he is left at home, so I take him with me whenever I can. I bought a basket that fits on my bike's handlebars, and he loves riding with the wind in his fur while smelling the fresh air. We mostly ride on rail trails in the Mid-Hudson Valley in New York. Bunny's favorite is the Walkway over the Hudson, where he intently watches the ships on the river. Unsurprisingly, a basket-riding dog gets lots of attention. Every once in a while I even hear someone humming the tune from *The Wizard of Oz*.

Diane & Bunny
HIGHLAND, NEW YORK ⟲ BUNNY_GATOR

YOU SPEND MORE ON YOUR DOG'S HAIR CARE THAN YOUR OWN.

My dog Wonton has, without a doubt, the most complex hair routine out of anyone in the family. He easily has more hair products than his human mom, and my wife and I didn't even own a blow dryer before him! I am solely in charge of Wonton's daily grooming, so I have become very familiar with a hairbrush. Every night as my wife falls asleep, Wonton snuggles up in my lap while we watch our favorite cartoons together, and I brush all the tangles and knots out of each ear and his belly. We also occasionally wrap his ears with wax paper and rubber bands to keep his hair away from his chomping mouth.

Maximilian & Wonton
BROOKLINE, MASSACHUSETTS
◎ WONTONSOUP_THE_PEKE

YOU TAUGHT YOUR MOTHER TO ACCEPT THE FACT THAT THE FASTEST WAY TO GET A RESPONSE FROM YOU IS TO TEXT YOU A PICTURE OF YOUR DOG.

Response time to my mom texting me *"How was your day?"*: anywhere from forty minutes to four hours.
Response time to my mom texting me a picture of my dog after a haircut: four seconds.

I will admit that sometimes I forget to respond to my mom's text messages, particularly regarding planning things that are not in the immediate future. We are opposites. My mom is a planner and I'm the last-minute type.

Over the years, she's discovered that if she wants my attention, all she has to do is text me a picture of our family dogs and I respond with lightning speed. It's actually pretty sneaky. She reels me in with a picture of the dog and then drops whatever plans she needs me to be aware of into the conversation.

Katie & Nellie
NEW YORK, NEW YORK

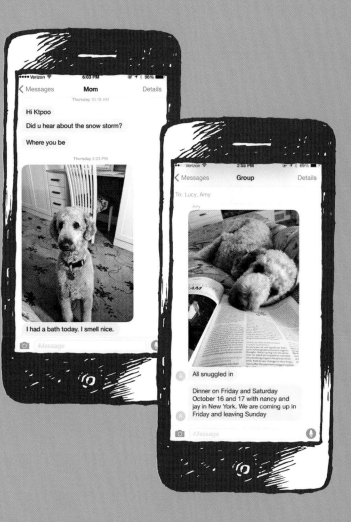

YOU HAD AN INSTAGRAM READY TO GO FOR YOUR DOG BEFORE YOU'D EVEN MET HIM.

Before I had a dog of my own, I wanted a reason to go up to dogs and pet them. I created my own Instagram account called ADogInTheApple and went around New York City asking dog owners, "Can I take a picture of your dog for my Instagram?" After about a year of this venture, my frequent encounters with dogs were still not satisfying my need for a furry friend. I decided it was time to adopt. After months of searching, I found Charlie. Though my family did not think it was the "right time" for me to get a dog, I knew he was the one. I rarely make quick decisions, but I was certain about him. Charlie is my sidekick and adventure partner. He is a pro on planes, trains, boats, and cars. He makes me laugh, brings people together, and overall makes me a better person. If I were to describe my perfect dog I would simply say, "Charlie!"

Perry & Charlie
NEW YORK, NEW YORK ⊙ ADOGINTHEAPPLE

YOU WILL CARRY YOUR FORTY-FIVE-POUND DOG DOWN A STEEP, ROCKY MOUNTAIN.

One beautiful autumn day, my husband and I went for a hike in the mountains with Blanca, our Standard Poodle. She started to limp, but when I checked her paws and pads nothing seemed to be amiss, so we continued. We took a few more steps and it was clear she was in distress. Without pausing, my husband picked Blanca up and we made our way down the trail. Blanca was fine the day after the hike, and we still wonder if she might have faked her injury for a free ride down the mountain!

Faith, Bryan & Blanca
FORT COLLINS, COLORADO
⦿ BLINKYBLANCA

BIRTHDAY

(burth-dey) n.

NO idea what this means, but basically one day you'll just be napping and all of a sudden your human straps a cone to your head and LIGHTS YOUR FOOD ON FIRE, and you start getting all these toys and treats. Then your friends come over and you have no idea what's happening, but you know that it's fun. Then it happens again in seven years.

YOU LET YOUR PUP CELEBRATE HIS BIRTHDAY WITH ALL OF HIS FURRY FRIENDS.

When Hudson turned one, we celebrated his Bark Day with his closest friends. We can't even remember the last time we threw birthday parties for ourselves.

Raquel, Neville & Hudson
NEW YORK, NEW YORK
HUDSONTHEGOLDENDOODLE

YOU STOP BY EVERY DOG STORE IN TOWN TO BUY THE CUTEST AND PRETTIEST BIRTHDAY CAKE FOR YOUR DOG, ONLY TO HAVE HIM DEMOLISH IT IN SECONDS.

Nacho's birthday is in August, and every year the celebration has grown longer. We went from celebrating for a day to a whole weekend, and this year we celebrated for an entire week. We're dreading what he'll expect next year.

Jenna & Nacho
BOSTON, MASSACHUSETTS 📷 NACHODOGG

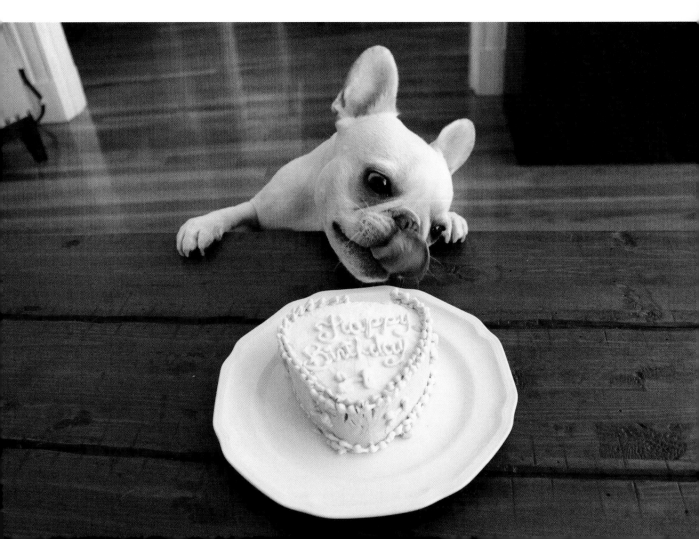

YOU THREW YOUR DOG A BIRTHDAY PARTY FIT FOR A FIRST GRADER.

We celebrated at a pet-friendly restaurant where we sang happy birthday to Tuukka and I handed out doggie party bags to her friends. Tuukka has a lot of allergies that prevent her from enjoying most dog foods and treats, so I ordered a special cake for her birthday party that she was able to enjoy with her furry friends.

Sara & Tuukka
COVINA, CALIFORNIA 📷 TUUKKATHEPIT

YOU TREAT YOUR DOG TO AN ANNUAL "BIRTHDAY BALL FIESTA."

Otto is obsessed with balls. Tennis balls, soccer balls, bouncy balls—if it is round and looks like a ball, Otto loves it! Each year on his birthday, our family throws him a huge "Birthday Ball Fiesta," where we humans find as many different balls as we can and hide them around our home. He goes absolutely nuts to see so many balls in one place, and the look of surprise and excitement he has each time he finds a new one never gets old.

Samantha & Otto
NEW YORK, NEW YORK 📷 OTTOGENE_FRENCHIE

YOU SPONTANEOUSLY TAKE A SEVEN-HOUR TRIP TO THE BEACH FOR YOUR DOG'S BIRTHDAY.

I had the weekend off work when Darcy's first birthday arrived, so on Saturday morning I woke up and spontaneously decided to drive to the beach! Darcy had never been to the beach before, but she loves water, so I knew she would like the ocean. Since it was off-season, she was able to frolic in the waves off leash and we played fetch to her heart's content. When we were tired out from the ocean and the sun, we went out for a birthday dinner at a dog-friendly restaurant, where she was given treats and lots of attention. Although it was a seven-hour round-trip drive, it was well worth it to celebrate my special pup and her big day.

Megan & Darcy
GIBSONVILLE, NORTH CAROLINA
THEDAILYDARCY

YOU MAKE SURE THAT EVERY YEAR IS YOUR DOG'S BEST BIRTHDAY.

For Lilo's first birthday I gave her a cute hat and put up a birthday banner. For her second birthday I went a step further and bought a pupcake and birthday toys! Lilo's third birthday and beyond are sure to be just as memorable.

Khoa & Lilo
SAN DIEGO, CALIFORNIA
LILOTHEWELSHCORGI

YOU NOT ONLY TREAT YOUR DOGS ON THEIR BIRTHDAYS, BUT ALSO TREAT DOGS IN NEED.

I haven't had a big celebration that included presents or a cake for my birthday in a while, but I make sure to treat my pups for their birthday celebrations. For Terra's birthday she got a cache of dog chews including buffalo ears and bully sticks; Kronos got a few new collars; and Bella got her Trick Dog Champion Title, a collar, a raw turkey neck, a cow hoof chew, and rawhide.

We've also recently started a tradition of donating to a nonprofit organization in honor of each birthday. For Kronos's birthday this year we donated to DreamChaser Horse Rescue and the Ian Somerhalder Foundation.

Tiffany, Bella, Terra & Kronos
SIERRA VISTA, ARIZONA
TIFFANYSDIAMONDDOGS

YOU WILL PARADE YOUR DOG AROUND IN A NOBLE CHARIOT THAT KEEPS GETTING BIGGER AND BIGGER.

My husband and I live in downtown Dallas, where we find it is easier and more fun to get around on a Vespa. When we brought Nelson home in April 2013, we took him riding almost immediately. We started by letting him ride in a small bag between us. When he outgrew the bag, we attached a basket to the back of the Vespa. And when he got too big for that, we found a sidecar! He knows that riding means brunch on patios, lots of people giving him kisses, and wind in his fur. When we get our helmets off the shelf, he jumps up and runs for the door. We love Nelson so much and can't imagine life without him. He's made riding our Vespa a million times more fun!

Genesis, James & Nelson
DALLAS, TEXAS
 NELSONTHEGOLDENDOODLE

HOW TO KEEP YOUR SIDECAR SIDEKICK SAFE

Know your sidekick. Riding should be fun, but not all pups will enjoy it. Do what you can to start slow and make the ride enjoyable for your sidekick. Give them lots of treats and love, and take them on rides to places they will enjoy!

Know your city streets. Remember to pay close attention to road signs, streetlights, and crossroads. Try to stay clear of really busy areas where cars tend to drive fast.

Doggles. The safety gear of choice by all other sidekicks. Your pup's eyes should be kept safe from the wind and sun with UV-protective goggles.

Be safe! Always make sure your lights work on both your ride and the sidecar. Never be afraid to use your horn liberally and let other drivers know you're there. Know your city's laws and make sure your seat belts are safe and installed properly. Contact your local scooter guy to find out how to keep your scooter/sidecar safe and law-abiding.

Pack before you ride! Consider everything your sidekick will need during your travels. We never ride without a full pack of doggy poop bags, our travel water bowl, and LOTS of Nelson's favorite treats!

Have fun! Bonding with your sidekick through riding is one of the most enjoyable and fulfilling memories.

Genesis, Mother of Nelson

YOU SPEND YOUR LIFE HELPING A BLIND DOG.

I first saw Odie at the high-kill Chicago Animal Care and Control facility while picking up a guinea pig for adoption transport. I wasn't ready for a dog at the time, but I never forgot seeing him in his cage with a sign that read, "Blind."

Odie was eventually pulled from the pound by a pet store in my town doing rescue and ended up staying there for six months. I would visit to pick up cat supplies and he would be in a puppy pen bouncing neurotically and stressed, but I didn't fully register that he was the same pile of fluff I had met months earlier. I began talking to Odie in a soothing voice to try to calm him while putting my hand on his back so he would relax and lie down whenever I would visit with him. I knew this was not the place for him, so I adopted him. Once he was home I remembered him from CACC and I knew we were destined for each other.

I consider Odie my PhD in animal communication. I had never had a dog before and actually spent most of my life being afraid of them. So I guess it makes sense that my first dog would be a high-maintenance, blind dog of questionable background. We now live in Las Vegas and have traveled together all over the country. He has seen me through jobs, speaking engagements, starting my own business, a new relationship, buying a house, and traveling. I love him endlessly.

Alicia & Odie
HENDERSON, NEVADA
ODIESEYES.COM

YOU THEMED YOUR BEDROOM SET AROUND YOUR DOG'S STYLISH STAIRS SINCE THE BED IS MORE HIS THAN YOURS.

Tucker has a big personality, so I knew he needed bedroom stairs to match. Once we found these stairs we knew they were perfect for him! After putting them in our room we realized we needed to upgrade the bed set to match. Tucker owns our bedroom!

Sandra, Jeff & Tucker
CARLSBAD, CALIFORNIA 🔘 TUCKERSDOGZONE

YOU KEEP A PENNY THAT YOUR DOG SWALLOWED IN A JAR TO REMIND YOU HOW YOU WOULD SPEND YOUR LIFE SAVINGS AGAIN AND AGAIN TO KEEP YOUR DOG ALIVE.

I came home one day to find my seven-month-old, Arya, very sick and unable to eat. I wrapped her in her favorite blanket and cradled her in my arms as I rushed to the emergency clinic. The veterinarian who briefly examined her told me that she needed immediate care.

Tests revealed that Arya needed a blood transfusion right away. Her blood count was very low and she had swallowed something that needed to be extracted. The proposed treatment

was expensive and there was no guarantee that Arya would survive. I didn't have the money and had no clue how I was going to get it, but I also knew that, in that moment, all that mattered was giving Arya every chance at life. I was told to prepare for the worst but hope for the best. They scheduled the surgery for the next morning, but late that night a nurse called to inform me that the doctor was headed in to perform the surgery right away. I was sick with worry and unable to sleep.

I shared Arya's story with her Instagram community, and the outpouring of support overwhelmed me. People from all over the world stayed up with me, leaving comments of hope, prayer, and love. They gave me strength and even created the hashtag #warriorprincess.

Two hours later, a vet tech assisting in Arya's surgery texted me a picture of the mysterious object in Arya's belly: a copper penny with a hole eroded at its center. We called it the million-dollar penny. Although I spent a pretty penny to extract this million-dollar penny, I would pay all the money in the world to keep my warrior princess by my side.

Eileen & Arya
GROVELAND, FLORIDA 📷 REINA.JAX.ARYA

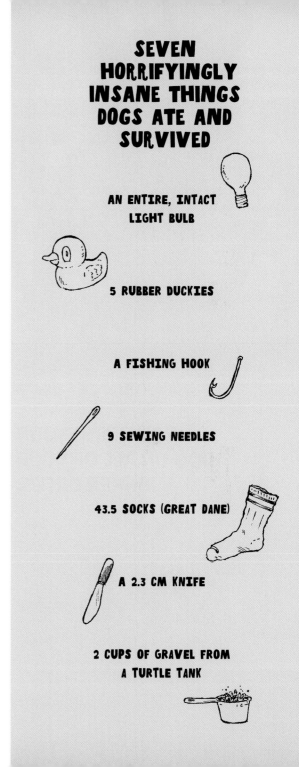

SEVEN HORRIFYINGLY INSANE THINGS DOGS ATE AND SURVIVED

AN ENTIRE, INTACT LIGHT BULB

5 RUBBER DUCKIES

A FISHING HOOK

9 SEWING NEEDLES

43.5 SOCKS (GREAT DANE)

A 2.3 CM KNIFE

2 CUPS OF GRAVEL FROM A TURTLE TANK

YOU BRING YOUR DOG ON ALL OF YOUR DINNER DATES.

When searching for a place to dine, my boyfriend and I filter places to eat with patio seating. If a place doesn't have patio seating, it may as well not exist. Many times, we tell the hostess it's a party of three—the two of us and our dog, Ninja. During our meal, Ninja sits with us at the table on a chair. When there is no chair, he will give you a death stare until he's on one. On one occasion, the restaurant was out of chairs, but a high chair was available so a high chair it was.

Cindy & Ninja
SAN JOSE, CALIFORNIA ◉ NINJEEEE

TWO DEWCLAWS DOWN

Restaurant: Joe's Tavern
Star rating: ★☆☆☆☆
Reviewer: Ninja

This was a truly demeaning dining experience. Like any dog, I expect a proper seat at the table when I take my hoomans out for a bite to eat. So imagine my shock and dismay when we arrived at our patio table and the hostess informed us that they had RUN OUT OF CHAIRS.

I thought it was a dumb joke, but she wasn't kidding. "What?! But you're a restaurant!" is what I would've said if I could talk. But I can't talk, so I fixed her with a death stare (which is what I normally do in these situations until a proper seat arrives). But they literally had no chairs, and none of the other patrons offered theirs. Instead, someone got the bright idea to bring out a HIGH CHAIR. You know, that weird tall thing drooly children sit in when they want to throw their food on the walls instead of eat it? Before I knew what was happening, I was scooped up and placed AGAINST MY WILL into a humiliating chair for a toddler hooman. Everyone kept staring at me. It was awful. I ate my food in silence and vowed to never return there. Unless they have a proper chair for me, in which case I will definitely return, because the food was actually pretty good.

YOU DON'T MIND IN THE LEAST THAT YOUR BIWEEKLY PAYCHECK CONTAINS A DOG TAX.

The Dog Tax, or what we affectionately call the HTF (Happy Tacoma Fund), actually started right when we rescued our dog Tacoma about four years ago. My boyfriend and I had just bought our current place eleven months before we rescued her, and we knew that we had to budget with a new pup in the family. So each biweekly paycheck had about $20 that went into the HTF, which made for a very happy Tacoma!

We're not so certain she knew back then, but like clockwork every destroyable toy she was given would be ready to be thrown out by the time the next $20 was available in her fund! With the arrival of her BarkBox subscription, we've been able to save a bit of HTF money for larger things she might need, like a new hockey jersey (since she is only able to fit into human sports jerseys).

Charlene, Pierre & Tacoma
VANCOUVER, BRITISH COLUMBIA 📷 COCOBUPS

"PLEASE, WE PREFER "ACCOUNTANT," NOT "BONE COUNTER.""

" I'LLLLLLLLLLL TAKE THAT, THANKS."

ACTUAL COST OF OWNING A DOG

Adoption Starter Kit

Adoption Fee $0-500
Spay/Neuter Surgery $50-200
Dog's Instagram account $0
Microchip $45
Puppy vaccinations $50-150
Newspaper subscription (to pee on) $100
Collar & leash $30
Food bowls $20
Crate $50
Little red wagon to pull your
puppy around everywhere $30
Shampoo and brushes $20
High-end orthopedic dog bed $125
The old couch pillow your dog
will choose to sleep on $4
Stain/odor removers $10
Dog toothpaste and toothbrush $15

Annual Expenses

Food $480
Toys $120
Matching Han Solo and Princess
Leia Halloween costumes $75
Flea and Tick meds $120
Heartworm meds $60
Customized dog-safe birthday cake
with dog's face on it $50
Poop bags $60
Treats $60
Okay, fine, actual treats budget..... $600
Annual routine pet exam $45-200
Annual routine "skip a week of work
because your dog is so cozy and you
just can't leave the couch" $500

Potential Annual Expenses

Emergency vet trip $0-3000
Emergency vet trip and it
turns out it was just gas........ $0-100
Teeth cleaning......................... $400
Replacement of chewed-up
underwear and mysteriously
vanished socks......................... $67
Pet sitting $25/night
Dog training $40/hour
Replacement of stolen lunches $7/sandwich

Optional Expenses

Pet insurance $35/month
Grooming.................................. $30-90
Literally The PERFECT dog
sweater $25
Pet license $30/year
Winning eBay bid for that
nearly irreplaceable squeaky
panda toy that your dog is
obsessed with $39

Estimated Average Cost per Year $2,858

Estimated Average Cuddles
per Year   31,697

TRAVEL

(trav·el) n.

When your human puts you in a bumpy machine for a while so that you can poop in a place you've never pooped before. IT'S AWESOME.

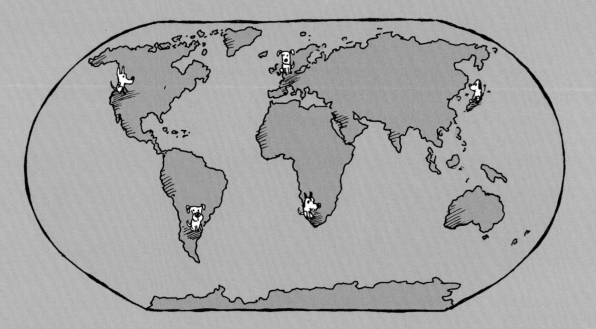

YOU GET YOUR DOG A PET PASSPORT.

When we drive, my German Shepherd, Kayla, sits upright, her nose pressed up against the window, watching the world go by. She loves the car so much that she drags me down city streets to wherever it's parked, toward any car that looks vaguely similar, or really any car at all, in hopes of going on a new adventure.

Together we have traveled more than twenty-eight thousand miles together. With her passport, she's flown over the Atlantic Ocean three times. We've taken trains and boats across England and driven more than ten thousand miles on I-80. A well-traveled pup, she's clocked up a few thousand more miles than the circumference of the world in her six years of life.

Dan & Kayla
NEW YORK, NEW YORK

CAR RIDE (kar rïd) n.

The best puppin' thing ever. Your jowls flap in the wind and your fur blows around in your face and you go very fast and oh, it's just the greatest. Buckle your seat belts, though. Safety is impawtant.

YOU GIVE YOUR VACATION DAYS TO YOUR DOG.

My husband and I love Kingsley and Sailor so much that we took time off from work and planned an entire vacation that revolved around them! We took a road trip up Pacific Coast Highway staying in Carmel-by-the-Sea, the most dog-friendly town in America. We stayed at the Cypress Inn, where dog blankets, bowls, and treats are provided. We did a lot of research finding all of the best attractions, trails, parks, stores, and restaurants along our road trip where our pups would be welcome. It brings me and my husband so much joy to see Kingsley and Sailor living the doggie dream.

Cheryl, Kingsley & Sailor
COSTA MESA, CALIFORNIA ⊙ KINGSLEYANDSAILOR

YOU FLY YOUR DOG TO THE BIG APPLE TO SEE THE COUNTRY'S BIGGEST CHRISTMAS TREE.

I have a few friends who live in New York City, so I decided to show Lilo the Big Apple during the holiday season. We enjoyed seeing the city covered in festive decorations and even got to treat Lilo to the giant Christmas tree in Rockefeller Center! (And no, she didn't pee on it!)

Khoa & Lilo
SAN DIEGO, CALIFORNIA
LILOTHEWELSHCORGI

YOU TAKE YOUR DOG TO EUROPE TO MEET THE POPE.

I loved bringing Toast to Europe! She adored Rome and desperately wanted to meet the pope but he wasn't in the city at the time, so we met the mini-pope. Toast and Mini-Pope had an amazing time around Rome, visiting the Colosseum, the Vatican and the Spanish Steps. But Toast didn't really care about the monuments—she was mostly concerned with the prosciutto.

Katie & Toast
NEW YORK, NEW YORK ⬤ TOASTMEETSWORLD

TOP FIVE

DESTINATIONS FOR DOG LOVERS AROUND THE WORLD

5. TOKYO, JAPAN. There are cafés in Tokyo that cater exclusively to your fuzzbutts, including a fancy faux garden and menus carrying a variety of dog-friendly food.

4. CAPE TOWN, SOUTH AFRICA. With its world-renowned beaches, Cape Town is hard to ignore. Enjoy a beautiful breezy sunset walk on the beach with only your pup love for company. It doesn't get better than this.

3. BUENOS AIRES, ARGENTINA. Three million humans, five hundred thousand dogs. That's how friendly Buenos Aires is. Pups are welcome practically anywhere, and this is apparent by the many businesses that bear pet-friendly signs.

2. AMSTERDAM, NETHERLANDS.* Amsterdam is EXTREMELY pet-friendly as it's packed with hotels, restaurants, cafés, and bars that cater to dogs and their humans. What's even better? Pups of any size are allowed on the train for three euros and on all other public transportation for free!

1. PORTLAND, OREGON. In this dog-loving city, there's something to do for everyone. Love adventure? Take off with your dog on one of the many hiking trails. Prefer something low-key? Grab a drink at an outdoor bar with your pooch in tow.

The Netherlands is the only country in the world with a political party aimed at improving animal well-being. The party is aptly called "Party for the Animals."

YOU DROVE TWELVE HOURS STRAIGHT ON A WHIM TO SAVE A DOG YOU KNEW WAS YOURS.

After months of searching online for a rescue dog, I discovered Charlie and instantly fell in love. When I learned about her horrible living conditions, I knew it was my mission to save her. My mom, who is also an animal lover, agreed to make the twelve-hour drive with me, so we drove through the night from New York to Indiana. We arrived to find Charlie living in a home with about sixty other neglected dogs. I notified the authorities of the conditions of this place, which no one should call a "rescue," and it was shut down permanently. All of the dogs were relocated to various no-kill shelters.

Out of this entire ordeal, I was able to grab Charlie. I took her to the closest gas station bathroom and bathed her in the sink. I promised that scrawny, scared puppy that from then on, she would lead an amazing life, full of love and joy. I take her everywhere and introduce her to people and experiences all over the country. Charlie is a miracle dog—it's a miracle that I found her and a miracle that she turned out to be a healthy, amazing dog who makes everyone around her smile.

Paige & Charlie
NEW YORK, NEW YORK ⊙ PUPPYNAMEDCHARLIE

YOU CARRY A BAG OF ROTISSERIE CHICKEN ON YOUR WALKS IN CASE OF AN IMPROMPTU PHOTO SHOOT.

There are so many beautiful places for photos here on the Oregon coast, so I'm always on the lookout for photo opportunities with Spock, my stubborn Dachshund. He likes most dog treats, but loves Costco rotisserie chicken the most. There is nothing he wouldn't do for a piece of chicken, so I started bringing a small bag of it on our walks. I have learned the best times to get the biggest chicken fresh out of the roaster and collected many recipes for what to do with the leftovers.

Sally, Chris & Spock
HAMMOND, OREGON ◉ MINISPOCK

YOU STAGE STRIKING WILDLIFE PHOTO SHOOTS TO LIONIZE YOUR TEACUP YORKIE'S ROOTS.

I have always been fascinated by the fact that Peppermint, my tiny two-and-a-half-pound Yorkie, likely shares 99 percent of her DNA with a gray wolf. So I staged a photo series that explores her wild side, with images shot in the style of a nature photographer capturing a feral animal in their natural habitat juxtaposed with the anthropomorphic elements we tend to place on our companion animals. Typical with my photography style, there is also an element of whimsy present in this series.

Alana, Dexter & Peppermint
TORONTO, ONTARIO DEXTERSRUFFLIFE

TIMELINE:
HISTORY OF DOG EVOLUTION

LEFTOVERS!

19TH CENTURY — DOG BREEDING EXPLODED, WITH MANY OF THE MOST RECOGNIZABLE BREEDS ROUNDING INTO FORM: THE LABRADOR RETRIEVER, THE GERMAN SHEPHERD, THE YORKIE, AND MORE.

ABOUT 5,000 YEARS AGO — DOGS BEGAN TO MAKE THEIR MARK ON HUMAN CULTURE—ANUBIS, AN EGYPTIAN GOD WITH A DOG FOR A HEAD, MAKES HIS FIRST APPEARANCE.

ABOUT 9,000 YEARS AGO — THE SALUKI, ONE OF THE FIRST FULLY DOMESTICATED BREEDS DELIBERATELY CREATED BY HUMANS, WAS BRED IN EGYPT. THE PHARAOH HOUND FOLLOWED (4,000 YEARS AGO), THEN THE IBIZAN HOUND (3,000 YEARS AGO).

10,000–14,000 YEARS AGO — AN ALTERNATE TIMELINE FOR THE DOMESTICATION OF DOGS, POSSIBLY BEGINNING IN CENTRAL ASIA, ACCORDING TO SOME STUDIES.

18,000–32,000 YEARS AGO — THE DOMESTICATION OF DOGS IN EUROPE, ACCORDING TO SOME STUDIES.

UP TO 40,000 YEARS AGO — THE ANCESTRAL DOG AND THE ANCESTRAL MODERN GRAY WOLF DIVERGED FROM A COMMON ANCESTOR.

40 MILLION YEARS AGO — RISE OF THE FIRST RECOGNIZABLE DOGS, THE BIOLOGICAL FAMILY CANIDAE. THEY SPLIT INTO THREE SUBFAMILIES: HESPEROCYONINAE, BOROPHAGINAE, AND CANINAE. ONLY CANINAE EXIST TODAY.

65 MILLION YEARS AGO — ORIGIN OF *MIACIS COGNITUS*, A SMALL, WEASEL-LIKE ANIMAL THAT LIVED IN TREES AND ATE INSECTS, BELIEVED TO BE THE ORIGINAL ANCESTOR OF DOGS.

YOU ARE A FULL-TIME, ROUND-THE-CLOCK NURSE FOR YOUR DOG.

Sadie is so small and fragile that when she broke her only front leg, my husband and I thought we were going to lose her. We had to give her an IV from home for almost a week. We would pin the IV bag to the wall to allow it to drip. We were full-time round-the-clock nurses for her until she healed. Even the vet wasn't sure she would ever walk again.

But she did. After her surgery, she didn't walk for at least a month, but one of us was with her at almost all times. We had a slinged harness specially made for her that helped us support her during physical therapy and trips to the bathroom. After all the time and care we put into Sadie's rehabilitation, she was not only able to walk again, but run, too!

The best part of Sadie's story is receiving e-mails from war veterans, people with depression or cancer, amputees, and others with disabilities who have reached out to tell us how much of an impact she's had on them. No matter how much is thrown her way, she is still the happy, treat-obsessed Chihuahua she always has been.

Liz & Sadie
DURHAM, NORTH CAROLINA SADIETRIPAWD

YOU RECOGNIZE THAT EVERY TIME YOU TRY TO BINGE-WATCH NETFLIX, YOU END UP WATCHING YOUR DOG INSTEAD.

No matter the time of day or night, the instant the TV goes on Brie believes that's her call to steal the spotlight. She'll grab a ball or a squeaky toy or just stare up longingly until my boyfriend and I take our eyes off of what's happening on the screen and pay attention to her every want and need.

In between gasping and shouting at the drama happening on the television and live-tweeting every moment of every episode, we appease Brie by tossing non-squeaky toys (we can't miss the dialogue!) down the hall for her to fetch until she tires out. When she's vying for our attention, she's usually trying to get her paws on our bowl of popcorn. She'll get right in our face and stare (and stare and stare) until we toss her a few kernels. If we have an exceptionally long TV marathon, she'll eventually lie down beside us on the couch, but not before crawling on top of us—and inevitably stepping on the remote. Before circling for minutes on end to find the perfect spot under the blanket, she licks our faces, demanding acknowledgment of her presence. Regardless of her shenanigans and interruptions, we wouldn't want to consume drama and comedy any other way.

Sean, Ray & Brie
SAN FRANCISCO, CALIFORNIA
BONJOURBRIE

More than you might think! When you and your pup settle down for a night of hard-hitting news (or, more likely, a *House Hunters* marathon), your dog is essentially seeing a lower-quality version of the images onscreen. They can discern shapes and movements, and they even know when an animal, like another dog, appears onscreen. Your pup's brain is also capable of processing imagery faster than yours, so modern advances like high-definition TV and faster frame rates make it even easier for dogs to appreciate the small screen.

A dog's ability to perceive color is limited, however, because of "dichromatic vision"—that is, their eyes detect only two of the three primary colors, and are therefore restricted to a yellow and blue spectrum. Despite this, nothing can stop you and your dog from enjoying another relaxing night in . . . and if you can, turn that TV to HD for your pup's optimal viewing pleasure!

YOU TREAT YOUR DOG TO ANTLERS THREE TIMES HIS SIZE.

Little Man is a thirty-seven-pound Puggle who believes he's a Mastiff. His favorite chew toys are moose antlers. In order to match the size he believes he is, I usually get him antlers that are rated for dogs at least twice his size. For his birthday, he was gifted antlers that weighed four pounds.

Jacky & Little Man
ROSCOE, NEW YORK

YOU TAKE YOUR DOGS TO THE PARK EVERY DAY BEFORE SUNRISE TO KEEP THEM SAFE.

SHE'S SHY.

I used to take my dogs to the park at normal daytime hours until one of them was attacked by an unsupervised dog. Since then, I've started going to the park really early to ensure my dogs' safety. For the last six years, my weekend visits to the park have started right before sunrise. Although I can't see the ball or my dogs, they love their alone time at the park and I love watching the sunrise with them. After our park adventure, we come home for a well-deserved nap before starting the rest of our day.

Randall, Benny & Carter-man
TAMPA, FLORIDA

YOU KNOW THAT YOUR SOCIAL CALENDAR IS REALLY JUST YOUR DOG'S SOCIAL CALENDAR.

Ever look at your calendar and realize your life belongs to your dog? Instead of drinks with coworkers, we go to dog-centric yappy hours. Brunch with friends? Sure, as long as we dine at a dog-friendly restaurant! With Potato in our lives, it's rare for us to stay home on the weekends, let alone weeknights. We've met more people in NYC in our first year with him than we have in the five years we've lived here. Potato is the happiest when he's surrounded by other dogs and people and because of him, we are too.

Tracy & Potato McTater
NEW YORK, NEW YORK ⬤ POTATO_MCTATER

August 2015

◼ Humans ◼ Potato

1 sat 10am Playdate w/ Koki
2 sun 9am Grocery Delivery
3 mon
4 tues
5 weds 12pm Annual Vet Exam
6 thurs
7 fri
8 sat Potato Gotcha Day Picnic
9 sun 11am Pug Meetup
10 mon
11 tues
12 weds 8pm Dinner and Drinks
13 thurs
14 fri
15 sat 7pm Date Night
16 sun

17 mon
18 tues 5pm Dentist Appointment
19 weds
20 thurs
21 fri
22 sat 10am Itty Ralphie Playdate
23 sun 7pm Dinner w/ Fam
24 mon 5pm Dinner at Scruffy's
25 tues
26 weds
27 thurs 7pm Seattle Small dog meetup
28 fri
29 sat Sleepover at daycare
30 sun

Notes

Refill heartworm/flea/tick
Schedule Grooming for Sept
Renew webcam subscription
Schedule haircut
Drop off donations
Order kibble and chews
Finalize Shih tzu Meetup

September

sun	mon	tues	weds	thur	fri	sat
		1	2	3	4	5
6	7	8	9	10	11	12
13	14	15	16	17	18	19
20	21	22	23	24	25	26
27	28	29	30			

YOU SHARE THE MOST IMPORTANT MOMENTS OF YOUR LIFE, GOOD AND BAD, WITH YOUR DOG.

My dog, Scarlett, has been with me for some of the toughest times in my life as I watched my parents age. Every time I visited my dad in the nursing home, Scarlett was with me because she brought him such happiness and joy. The other residents, nursing staff, and visitors watched in disbelief as she marched straight toward his room. The day my father passed, Scarlett was there with my daughter and her friend. She captured this photo of him holding her just three hours prior.

Recently, my ninety-four-year-old mom became a long-term resident at the same nursing home. As soon as the elevator doors open, just like with my dad, Scarlett charges down the hall and leaps into my mom's lap. Scarlett helps her cope with her physical and psychological pains, bringing her relief in a time of need. Knowing that she has brought peace to my parents brings tears to my eyes. Scarlett will remain very special to me for the rest of my life...and beyond.

Marina & Scarlett
QUEENS, NEW YORK

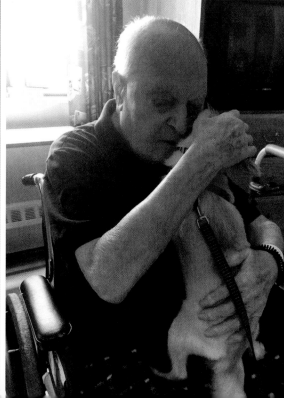

YOU CONTINUE TO LEARN YOUR GREATEST LIFE LESSONS FROM YOUR DOGS.

Bella and Beau are my life, my smile, my happiness, my family, my lucky charms, and my whole world. They taught me how wonderful it is to be myself, and they made me see that even when the whole world is collapsing, there is always a reason to be happy. When I see their eyes looking at me, it's like a miracle happens and I find my strength again.

Every day I wake up and watch as Bella and Beau embrace the new morning as if it's going to be great. They don't look back, and they don't worry about the future. I don't even remember what my life was like before having them because they've opened my eyes. I love them for the thousands of reasons they give me to smile. They taught me that love speaks to the soul and sings to the heart.

Alexandra, Bella & Beau
ATHENS, GREECE 📷 BELLALOVESBEAU

YOU AND YOUR DOG OWN FIFTY MATCHING OUTFITS THAT YOU WEAR TO DOG EVENTS AROUND NYC.

I rescued Holly about three years ago, and even though I was a recent college grad living in a tiny studio, I knew she would live a positively fabulous life. Holly gets a holistic home-cooked diet, has private babysitters come when I have nights out, and of course sleeps in my bed. But the thing we're probably best known for is our clothes. Holly and I have over fifty matching outfits, which we wear to dog events across New York City.

It started out innocently enough. I thought mommy-and-me Ralph Lauren polos were too cute to pass up for Holly's first birthday. We wore them to a couple of events, and people started to notice. The rest, as they say, is history. We now do an annual professional photo shoot. Despite the side eyes we might get from some, there is nothing better than the pure joy Holly and I both get from our adventures in matching outfits. She whines with excitement when we suit up to go out, and she knows how to strut her stuff in a mountain of tulle better than most prima ballerinas.

Mary & Holly Golightly
NEW YORK, NEW YORK
 LITTLEHOLLYSBIGWORLD

WELL, THAT'S EMBARRASSING.

YOU STARTED AND MANAGE AN INSTAGRAM ROCK BAND WITH YOUR DOG AS THE DRUMMER.

While I was out shopping, I saw a black T-shirt with a drum set on it and knew it would be perfect for Axel's next venture. I brought part of my son's drum set downstairs, borrowed my husband's drumsticks, and used my sunglasses to make my sweet bully a rocker. After taking the perfect picture, I posted to his Instagram account that #AxelsAwesomeBand was in need of singers, dancers, musicians, managers, promoters, drivers, and security. Axel had tons of dog friends, a cat, and even a gerbil post their pictures and dancing videos, all wanting to be in #AxelsAwesomeBand! Now that we have our members, we "perform" at Instagram parties by using Flipagram photos of the band and a party song handpicked for each pup's personality or birthday theme. We even sing carols at Christmas!

Melanie & Axel
BARTLETT, TENNESSEE
AXEL_THEAWESOME_ENGLISHBULLDOG

AXEL

BONO THE FRENCHIE

BRODALICIOUS

GUS THE ENGLISH BULLDOG

CHESTER'S WORLD

DECESARE SALAD

YOU GLADLY SPEND YOUR AFTERNOONS RAKING PILES OF LEAVES FOR YOUR DOG TO JUMP IN.

Leo has loved chasing leaves around the yard for as long as we've known him. When my husband gets home from work, he lies on the ground, covered with leaves. Then I let Leo back outside, but he is not easily fooled! He knows immediately that his dad is hidden in the pile. We spend entire afternoons standing in the cold, just watching Leo having the time of his life chasing leaves. It is truly such a joy to see him so genuinely happy over something so simple.

Danielle & Leo
DANIELSVILLE, PENNSYLVANIA
LEO_THE_BOXER_MASTIFF_

YOU TRY TO MAKE YOUR DOG A DIE-HARD BASEBALL FAN, JUST LIKE YOU.

Every year my husband and I take Ariel to the Pups in the Park event at Dodger Stadium. We ordered a custom pink jersey for her to wear and always arrive at least four hours early to be sure to get a prime spot in the pup parade on the field. For the pregame festivities, we carry Ariel to our favorite spots on the field. In ninety-degree weather, the asphalt can be extremely hot so we carry Ariel around as we enjoy the pregame festivities and once the game starts, we keep her cool with wet towels and treat after treat as we enjoy the game.

Katrina, Eric & Ariel
LOS ANGELES, CALIFORNIA ◉ ITSAWEENIEWORLD

IS "BASEBALL" ANOTHER WORD FOR "HEAVEN"?

YOU SAW ONE FACEBOOK POST OF YOUR NAMELESS DOG, FELL IN LOVE, AND THEN FLEW HIM OVER INTERNATIONAL BORDERS TO BRING HIM HOME.

When I came across Hero in a Facebook rescue group, it looked like he had given up on life. With bite wounds all over his legs, a skin infection, and mange, he'd been placed in quarantine in a cold cell where the public couldn't see him. His brown eyes pierced my soul and I knew he was meant for more. I reached out to everyone I knew, desperately seeking a way to help him. Within the hour, a rescue group in the Vancouver area pulled Hero out of the shelter and he was on his way to the vet. He was in boarding for two weeks until he

was healthy enough to travel to Canada, so in the meantime, we ran an online auction to raise funds for his care.

He has now turned into my hero and reminds me daily of how much he loves me. His is a true story of what love can do for the underdog.

Melissa & Hero
VANCOUVER, BRITISH COLUMBIA
 THEVANDOGDIARIES

YOU HAVE FREQUENT LABRAJEWDLE CELEBRATIONS.

Our family is culturally Jewish and observes major holidays. My wife and I jokingly said our dog Monty had a bris when he was neutered. For Yom Kippur, he fasted for the day (sneaking in a treat when needed). On Rosh Hashanah, there were Orthodox Jews in the park, where we said a prayer together. He got a present every night of Chanukah, and even played dreidel with other Doodle friends. On some Friday nights during Shabbat we give him a yarmulke and feed him a piece of challah. He is a true Labrajewdle, but he's not kosher, as bacon is one of his favorite foods. Monty is still a puppy, but we are planning his bark mitzvah when he turns thirteen in dog years (about twenty-two months in human years). Shalom!

Matt, Marni & Monty
BROOKLYN, NEW YORK 📷 MONTYDOODLEDOO

YOU MAKE YOUR DOG A PART OF YOUR FAMILY'S IMPORTANT HOLIDAY TRADITIONS.

On each of the eight nights of Chanukah, Rosenberg and I follow the traditions of the holiday. He puts on his tallis and his yarmulke, we light a candle, and he gets a present. He finishes the evening out by playing with his dreidel. Every morning I make potato latkes, which Rosenberg insists on eating with sour cream instead of applesauce. Rosenberg's father is Hassidic, so it is very important to us that he identifies as a Jewish K9.

Chantal & Rosenberg
BROOKLYN, NEW YORK 📷 ROSENBERGTHEDOG

YOU DROVE SIX HOURS SO YOUR DOG COULD GIVE HIS APPROVAL OF THE NEWEST MEMBER OF YOUR FAMILY.

Elvis is my two-year-old hilarious little potato, and after bringing him into my life, I instantly wanted a second clown dog. We drove six hours to meet a four-month-old pup, praying that Elvis would accept her. As soon as we walked through the door, there was an instant connection and they were in love. We named her Coco Bean. Elvis was always a happy guy, but when we brought her home it was like something awakened inside him. They sleep together, play together, are partners in crime, and also love to snuggle on the same lap, which makes for a very overcrowded lap!

Jessica, Elvis & Coco Bean
BOSTON, MASSACHUSETTS
ELVIS_THEFRENCHBULLDOG

MY LI'L DOGGIES DON'T GITALONG...

FAMILY COUNSELING

YOU BUY A CAMPER SO YOUR DOG CAN TRAVEL THE WORLD WITH YOU.

I bought a camper for my dog, Candy Rose, because she is my best friend and I want her by my side on all of life's adventures. I didn't want to board Candy and I had a difficult time finding pit bull–friendly outdoor getaways. Then an idea came to me: I could buy a camper and park it at a permanent, dog-friendly campground. We would have the perfect place to experience nature, relax, and take walks.

To make sure Candy Rose had plenty of space, I bought a thirty-three-foot travel trailer. She loves the fireplace and treats the separate bedroom as her domain. We visit the campground almost every weekend in the warmer months and even, on occasion, brave the cold. Including Candy Rose on my weekend retreats was the best decision I ever made.

Michele & Candy Rose
PEORIA, ILLINOIS

YOU LET YOUR HUSBAND JOIN THE MARINES AND SERVE ON TWO TOURS AS LONG AS YOU GOT TO HAVE THE DOG OF YOUR DREAMS.

When Jordan, my boyfriend of five years, decided to quit his job in finance and join the United States Marine Corps, I was concerned for his safety and wary of this drastic change in our lives. I told him I was on board with the decision under one condition: we get a puppy before his first deployment.

Two years, one huge move from New York City to tiny Surf City, North Carolina, one wedding, and one impending deployment later, on July 21, 2007, Jordan and I drove to a small suburb outside Charlotte and picked up the newest addition to our family in the form of a fourteen-pound ball of fur named "Hank the Deployment Puppy." A week later, Jordan deployed to the Middle East.

Hank and I were left in a sleepy beach town in the middle of nowhere to figure each other out and build our new life. I had never been a morning person, but

Hank had me out of bed early every morning and we went directly to the beach no matter the weather. Directly after I finished work in the evening, we went straight to the beach again.

Being a military spouse is challenging and there are moments of loneliness and frustration during a deployment. But Hank seemed to know every time I was down, and he would lift me back up by doing something hilarious or nuzzling up next to me and falling asleep. As Jordan would say, Hank was the E.T. to my Elliott. He seemed to double in size each night, going from fourteen pounds to eighty pounds in six months. When Jordan came home, Hank the little deployment puppy was a dog.

Hank and I went through two deployments together, and our Marine Corps days are behind us now. He finally stopped growing (at three years old) and

leveled out at a cool 170 pounds. We now have a little girl, who loves him almost as much as I do. At almost nine years old, he is slowing down a bit and his muzzle is getting a little gray, but his sweet puppy face is still the same and he rarely leaves my side. He still lays his head in my lap and purrs like a kitten, and he still chases birds when he gets the chance. The appreciation I have for what he has taught me about friendship, loyalty, and motherhood is endless...slobber and all.

Katie, Jordan & Hank
PHILADELPHIA, PENNSYLVANIA

YOU WAKE UP AT THE CRACK OF DAWN SO YOU CAN GIVE YOUR DOG AN HOUR AT THE "PRIVATE" BEACH.

Tazz is happiest wherever there is water and room to run, so naturally, he loves going to the beach. Our go-to beach gets crowded quickly, so we go around dawn in order to have the whole place to ourselves. He has the time of his life chasing seagulls, jumping over the tide, and running at full speed after his Frisbee. It may be early and mean that I need coffee to function for the rest of the day, but watching him at his happiest makes it all worth it.

Hannah & Tazz
MILWAUKEE, WISCONSIN ⬛ TAZZYDW2

YOU HAVE A NEW RELATIONSHIP WITH PEANUT BUTTER BECAUSE OF YOUR DOG.

Our rescue dog, Jack, had bounced around a few shelters and foster homes and had been recently surrendered when my wife and I met him. We adopted him and loved him and he immediately became very protective of us everywhere we went. His favorite defense was an attack posture with incessant barking. It was hard to even take him for walks.

At home, Jack loved to eat peanut butter and play fetch with tennis balls. We started to carry both items with us when we went out, and they became calming distractions for him. Peanut butter and tennis balls meant we were all safe. He now loves going to the park and meeting new friends on the street. And he still gets that same intense look in his eyes when he sees the peanut butter come out.

Mike & Jack
NEW YORK, NEW YORK 📷 PEANUTBUTTERJACK

YOU STITCH AND TAPE YOUR PUP'S FAVORITE TOYS BACK TOGETHER TO KEEP HIM HAPPY, EVEN THOUGH YOU HAVE ACCESS TO ALL THE DOG TOYS UNDER THE SUN.

WHAT IS THE TRUE MEANING OF "TOY"?

Every time my dog Gus destroys his favorite toys, I insist on piecing them back together. I'm actually the head of merchandising at Bark & Co. (BarkBox), so when I say that I have an exact replica of Gus's favorite toy that he just destroyed, I'm being entirely serious.

I'm sure it has something to do with immediate gratification, but I just hate to see Gus so let down. He should have his favorite toy whenever he wants it. Gus prefers a hand-me-down or gently used toy over the brand-new ones, like a child who refuses to wear anything but their favorite T-shirt even though they have ten other shirts that feel and look exactly the same. And since Gus is my son, I repair his favorite toy just like a parent peels the child's favorite T-shirt off to wash it as they sleep at night.

Melissa & Gus
NEW YORK, NEW YORK ☉ SUAVEGUSTAV

TIPS FROM THE EXPERT: HOW TO MAKE THE ULTIMATE DOG TOY

Making a good toy is a careful science; beyond taking material and durability into consideration, a perfect toy incorporates one or more of these key features:

PLAY STYLE

Does the toy fit styles of play that dogs love, like thrashing, tossing, snuggling, or chewing?

PREDATOR/PREY

Does a toy simulate a real relationship that dogs have with preylike critters in real life? *(i.e., our woolly mammoth plush)**

SQUEAKER/NOISE

Should it match the character of the toy or be intentionally different? *(i.e., the Dognald grunts; Bearded Lady giggles!)*

HUMOR/NOSTALGIA

We always imagine how a person will feel when they pick up a toy or open a BarkBox. How funny and adorable would it be to see a dog holding the toy in his/her mouth? *(ie: a poop emoji plush toy)*

*Check out some of these toys on BarkShop.com!

BY MELISSA, BARKBOX HEAD OF MERCHANDISING (AND GUS'S MOM)

YOU ALWAYS NEED YOUR DOG'S ADVICE, EVEN IF IT'S JUST AT THE MANICURIST.

Whenever I get my nails done, Blue is in my lap on snooze duty but periodically checks in to make sure I walk out of the salon looking glamorous. She has been known to choose the color with her little snout. In fact, the same day I got her, we first drove all the way from Pennsylvania to NYC with her, and then went straight to the nail salon. She was just a three-month old puppy then, snoozing on my lap.

Babba & Blue
NEW YORK, NEW YORK 📷 BLUE.OFFICIAL

YOU ARE TOTALLY OKAY WITH BEING KNOWN ONLY AS "LACEY'S MOM."

My boyfriend, Cameron, rescued our dog, Lacey, when she was about two years old, and ever since, I've gotten used to only being recognized for my dog. She has a high-pitched whine and unlimited energy and can bring a smile to anyone's face—and I've never gone anywhere without everyone immediately fawning over her. Our local nursery is dog-friendly and Lacey always leaves with a full belly of treats; one employee even offered dogsitting services to me because he is so charmed by her whenever she visits. In the past, I've gone there without her and had concerned employees ask if she was okay and wonder why she wasn't with us. She is a conversation starter and people stop in their tracks to greet her. In a world obsessed with technology it's easy to overlook the simple things that truly connect us—like a silly, smiley dog.

Sarah, Cameron & Lacey
HOUSTON, TEXAS
🄾 LACEY_RAWLINS

YOU HAVE YOUR DOG'S NAME AND PORTRAIT TATTOOED ON YOUR LEG.

After my granddad died, leaving the house became difficult. I have battled depression and anxiety throughout most of my life, and losing my best friend made it worse. I'd always wanted a dog, but my family moved constantly, making it difficult to have one. I decided it was time to get a companion since I now lived alone, with no plans of moving.

I picked up my Boycie in a matter of days, and it was as if he had been waiting for me. Words cannot describe how much he changed my life and helped me cope with my mental health issues. I wish assistance dogs for mental health patients were recognized more in

Austria, but luckily, he is able to accompany me nearly everywhere. Dogs are the most wonderful creatures to grace this planet, and I am thankful and happy to have a new best friend who has not only changed my life but made me a better person. Boycie has been such an important part of my recovery and life, so I decided to get his portrait tattooed on my leg so he will always stay by my side. We recently added another puppy to our family, a girl Maltese called Bubbles, and my life is now complete.

Arnela & Boycie
GRAZ, AUSTRIA

YOU MAKE SURE THAT YOUR DOG HAS A BED IN EVERY ROOM OF YOUR HOUSE.

Lulu has a bed in every room of the house because she never knows when she'll need a nap to survive an exhausting day of doing nothing. She is CEO of Napping, Inc., after all.

Bethany & Lulu
FIRESTONE, COLORADO  LULU.DA.BRAT

YOU FOUND YOUR DOG ON THE SIDE OF THE ROAD, TOOK OUT A LOAN TO SAVE HER LIFE, AND STILL KNOW THAT IT WAS THE BEST THING THAT EVER HAPPENED TO YOU.

I found Kyra, my Alaskan Malamute, hobbling on three legs and crying along the road outside Austin in July 2014. I was crying with her because I felt so bad seeing an animal so hurt. The phone number on her collar was disconnected, and we discovered she wasn't microchipped. X-rays showed us she had a bad break in her front leg. I decided to take out a loan to cover the cost of Kyra's surgery—and so began our life together.

Since finding Kyra, we have gone through three surgeries to repair her severely broken leg. As Kyra's leg healed after each surgery, we began going on short walks, which escalated to short swims, and finally twenty-minute walks three times a day. After each walk, I would massage her whole body with a handheld massager to relieve any stress that had built up because she wasn't able to use her fourth leg. For the full year that this process took, my whole life was put on hold so I could be with Kyra.

She is fully recovered now, and Kyra and I love to go on hikes and to dog parks together and see who can run up the hill faster. Sometimes we'll pack up the car and rent a cabin to get away in the woods together. She truly is my world. As unfortunate as it was finding each other under the circumstances, I could not have asked for a better gift in life than finding Kyra. I have sacrificed a lot for her, but words can't explain how much she has saved me more than I could ever save her.

Renata & Kyra
AUSTIN, TEXAS 📷 STORY OF TWO TAILS

YOU GAVE YOUR DOG THE CHANCE TO SURF AND NOW SHE BALANCES BOARDS AND LIVES.

I had planned for Ricochet to be a service dog for a person with a disability through the nonprofit I founded, but I guess she thought I said SURFice dog, because she jumped on a surfboard with a fourteen-year-old quadriplegic boy one day, and the rest is history. Since that day, she has been surfing as an assistive aide with people with disabilities, kids with special needs, wounded warriors, and veterans with PTSD.

What I've done out of a tremendous love for my dog is also based on a tremendous respect for all dogs. I think of the human-canine bond as a mutual partnership, and I believe dogs are on Earth to teach humans lessons. They are always communicating—we just have to listen. So what I do out of the love for my dogs is help others realize just how powerful and magical dogs are. If we listen to what they are saying, and give them the freedom to make their own decisions, we can learn monumental lessons from our pups.

Because I've been listening to Ricochet, my life has changed dramatically. She has taught me just how valuable a dog's perspective can be. I truly believe there is so much more for us to learn from dogs just like my Ricochet.

Judy & Ricochet
ESCONDIDO, CALIFORNIA 🄵 SURFDOGRICOCHET

YOU HAVE NO CHOICE BUT TO ACCEPT THAT YOUR DOG HAS AN INCREDIBLY SOPHISTICATED PALATE.

As Wellington's personal caterer, I've learned the following:

1. Fuji apples > all other apples

2. Asian pears > all other pears because crunchy and juicy > mushy and gross

3. Cut-up fruit = necessity. If we don't cut them up in small pieces he bites the large pieces in two, spits one half out, and crunches away on the first half, because this gourmet Doodle doesn't gulp food down in one bite.

4. Not all dog biscuits are created equal, which means I typically end up making him fresh biscuits!

Dora & Wellington
STATEN ISLAND, NEW YORK
⊙ DOODOFWELLINGTON

INTERESTING...BUT NOT EXACTLY WHAT I THOUGHT A CAT WOULD TASTE LIKE.

YOU TRAVEL WITH A SMALL CARDBOARD CUTOUT OF YOUR DOG.

My family traveled a lot when I was younger. The two things I missed most when we were away were my bed and my dog. I couldn't do anything about the bed, and fifty-pound, ill-trained Princess wasn't exactly a travel-friendly pup. One day I made a cardboard likeness of my favorite mutt and named her "To-Go Princess." To-Go Princess slept in a replica of the recycling bin she claimed as a bed the day we brought her home. My parents were a little alarmed when I started bringing To-Go Princess on the adventures real Princess missed, but she made my trips complete. Our dear Princess has since passed, making To-Go Princess even more special.

Annie & Princess
ST. LOUIS, MISSOURI
ANNIECOSBYBOOKS

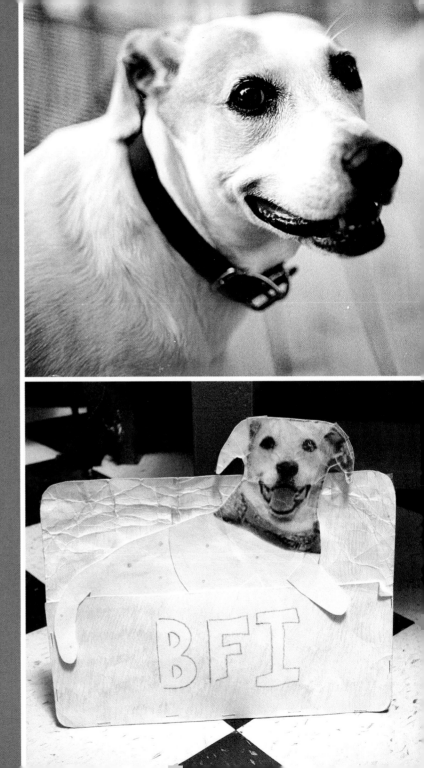

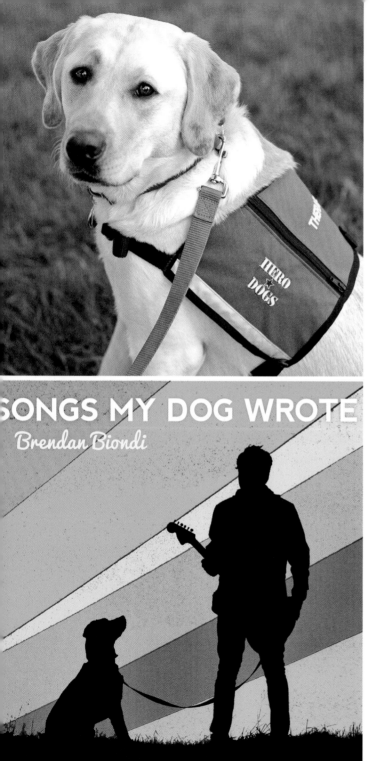

SONGS MY DOG WROTE

Brendan Biondi

YOU MADE A FULL-LENGTH ROCK ALBUM WITH YOUR DOG.

A few years ago, my partner, Christen, and I decided to volunteer with Hero Dogs, Inc., an organization that trains and places service dogs for veterans with disabilities. We ended up with a four-month-old yellow Labrador named Calvin whom we were responsible for guiding through service dog training. A year in, we discovered Calvin had severe allergies. His need for weekly allergy shots meant he no longer qualified as a service dog for a veteran.

After much thought, we decided it was best for us to adopt him. Today, Calvin is a certified therapy dog and makes visits to the Walter Reed National Military Medical Center and the Armed Forces Retirement Home in Washington, D.C. Throughout our journey, Calvin has taught me many valuable lessons and inspired my songwriting. Eventually, I had enough for a full-length rock album, *Songs My Dog Wrote*. Eleven of the twelve tracks are written from a dog's perspective, but the final track on the album is a lullaby I wrote for Calvin.

Brendan & Calvin
ELLICOTT CITY, MARYLAND 📷 HERODOGCALVIN

YOU ARE PREPARED TO STARE DOWN A BEAR JUST SO YOU AND YOUR DOG CAN GET HER DAILY TASTE OF NATURE.

Cali and I are both from Vancouver but are currently living in Fort McMurray for work. We live a couple of minutes' walk from an endless network of beautiful paved and dirt trails. In Vancouver, the bears are in the mountains, so we never encountered them, but in Fort McMurray, they are much more common. One of my biggest fears is coming across a bear, yet I go on the trails with Cali daily to keep her happy. It's "our place." I often carry bear spray on the longer trail walks for safety, but *every* time we round a corner or enter the trails it's the first thing on my mind. Despite the risks, Cali adores all the scents and smells of the outdoors and loves roaming the woods. As a puppy, she was so mesmerized at first by squirrels, then leaves, and now snow!

Caitlyn & Cali
FORT MCMURRAY, ALBERTA
PRINTSOFCALI

This town ain't big enough for the both of us!

YOU ARE GENUINELY OFFENDED WHEN YOU ENCOUNTER NON-DOG-FRIENDLY ESTABLISHMENTS.

If the dogs can't come, I won't even bother.

Lauren, Angel, Juliet, Murphy & Pepi
ALBUQUERQUE, NEW MEXICO 📷 WOOFWAGLOVE

YOU RESPONDED TO A SKETCHY CRAIGSLIST AD AND DROVE ACROSS THE STATE TO GET YOUR FUTURE DOG.

I first saw Frank on a sketchy Craigslist ad. The details on the ad read: "Need to get rid of Malti-Poo puppy TODAY." I had two initial thoughts: *First, what happens if they don't get rid of this precious fluff muffin today? And second, that is definitely not a Malti-Poo.* I grabbed a friend and drove to San Antonio to meet this pup at a Shell station. When we drove back to Austin, I had a new best friend.

Frank has that puppy head-tilt of curiosity that makes you smile no matter how many of your shoes he's destroyed in the hour, or how much toilet paper he has spread all over your apartment in a matter of seconds. Frank has become a celebrity pup around Austin and a regular at all the pup-friendly hangouts. Now, when I run into acquaintances, I am referred to as "Frank's mom." I seriously wonder if many of them know my real name, but that's fine because Frank is way cooler than I am.

Ali & Frank
AUSTIN, TEXAS

YOU CAMPAIGN TO REBRAND PIT BULLS TO TRY TO MAKE THE WORLD A KINDER PLACE FOR YOUR DOG.

Putting stuff on the head of my Pit Bull, Scout, snowballed slowly over the years. It was a great training tool and exercise of positive reinforcement and a fantastic outlet for my cheesy puns. When I started doing more than just treats (the first item was a roll of toilet paper), he sat there with such stoic concentration that I would have been stupid to pass up an opportunity to show off just how amazing, patient, and dedicated such a breed with a bad rap could be.

When I was given the opportunity to write a book starring Scout, I wanted to be able to scream from the mountaintops what an amazing breed the Pit Bull can be when given the proper care. To be able to display such lighthearted photos with a strong message that was simple enough to be appreciated by kids was a dream come true. As corny as it may sound, Scout's ability to exercise balance brought more balance and patience into my own life. He's taught me to be more selfless.

Jen & Scout
TORONTO, ONTARIO
STUFFONSCOUTSHEAD.COM

WHAT IS BREED-SPECIFIC LEGISLATION (BSL)?

Breed-specific legislation (BSL) refers to regulations that either ban or restrict specific kinds of dogs based on their appearance, typically because they are perceived as a "dangerous" class of dogs. This includes not only dogs that are identified as belonging to the breed but also any dogs that are seen as possessing "substantially similar" physical traits to the breed. BSL emerged from a growing public awareness of dog attacks on humans and other animals in the 1980s. Pit Bull–type dogs—and to a lesser extent Rottweilers, Dobermans, and German Shepherds—are primarily targeted with BSL. For example, in both Denver and Miami, the ownership of Pit Bulls is completely banned. Many expert dog groups as well as the Centers for Disease Control and Prevention (CDC) and the White House oppose BSL, and in the United States it is diminishing in practice.

WEDDINGS

(wed·dingz) n.

When two humans agree to sniff one butt
and one butt only fur the rest of their lives.

"YOU MAY NOW SNIFF THE BRIDE."

YOU PLAN YOUR ENTIRE WEDDING AROUND YOUR DOGS BECAUSE, LET'S BE HONEST, THEY'RE BASICALLY YOUR CHILDREN BORN OUT OF WEDLOCK.

My then-fiancée and I rented out a farm/inn for our wedding that expressly allowed dogs on the premises (even in the bridal suite). Our save-the-date cards had our dogs on them, and our invitations had customized art of our dogs. We incorporated our dogs into the ceremony as much as we possibly could because a wedding without them just wouldn't have been the same.

Ben, Suzanna, Guybrush & Hans Gruber
BROOKLYN, NEW YORK ⦿ HANSYANDBRUSH

YOU MADE YOUR DOG A PART OF YOUR WEDDING PROPOSAL.

My now-husband and I came home from our first-date-anniversary dinner to be greeted by our puppy Dexter with a ring attached to his collar. I didn't even see the ring at first and my husband had to practically point it out to me!

Theresa & Dexter
WALLA WALLA, WASHINGTON

CLEVER TIPS FOR INCORPORATING YOUR DOG INTO YOUR WEDDING

* Dress to impress. Show everyone how much your dog means to you by handcrafting them a floral crown or collar that coordinates with the bridal bouquets.

* Pupdate your dessert table with options for your four-legged family members like peanut butter cupcakes and carob cookies. Just make sure the human treats are kept well out of reach of prying puppy noses!

* If your venue doesn't allow dogs, it's a thoughtful touch to send guests home with keepsake doggie bags of homemade treats.

* You're obviously going to include your dog as a guest star in your engagement and wedding day photos, so take it a step further by setting up a photo booth where guests can pose with their pups!

* If you're not the registry type, share the love and opt to have guests donate to a pup-loving charity of your choice instead of bringing gifts.

YOU LANDED THE PERFECT FLOWER GIRL FOR YOUR WEDDING BEFORE YOU WERE EVEN ENGAGED.

When my then-boyfriend and I got engaged, we chose our dog Sneakers to be our flower girl before making any other decisions about the wedding. We even made sure to pick a venue that allowed dogs! Sneakers did an amazing job as the flower girl—as soon as she saw everyone waiting at the end of the aisle, she ran as fast as she could toward all of us to say hello. We're so happy Sneakers was there to help us celebrate!

Connie, Chris & Sneakers
SAN FRANCISCO, CALIFORNIA
📷 SNEAKERSTHECORGI

YOU RENTED YOUR OWN WEDDING DRESS, BUT HAD A CUSTOM WEDDING GOWN DESIGNED AND SHIPPED FROM ANOTHER COUNTRY FOR YOUR DOG.

When I got engaged, I knew that our three-year-old Cockapoo, Kiki, would be an integral part of our wedding day. I decided to rent my wedding dress and found it after an easy search. However, no dress, collar, or accessory was good enough for Kiki. I spent hours sketching a design and scoured Etsy in search of the perfect seamstress to create Kiki's dress. I finally found our seamstress, who lived in a different country! We spent months e-mailing back and forth before finalizing the design of

the dress. When it arrived, I could hardly contain my excitement! It was a beautifully hand-sewn silk piece, complete with a lace overlay and Swarovski crystal elements. The dress had been tailored to Kiki's exact body measurements and fit perfectly.

Allison & Kiki
OAKLAND GARDENS, NEW YORK
KIKITHEWONDERDOG

YOU HIRED SOMEONE TO DRIVE YOUR DOG THREE HOURS TO YOUR WEDDING VENUE FOR PRE-CEREMONY PICTURES.

While we were planning our summer wedding in Maine we knew there was no way the day would be complete without our one-and-a-half-year-old rambunctious Coonhound mix rescue named Scout. Undeterred, we hired a not-so-cheap dog concierge service to pick her up from Massachusetts and drive her three hours to the wedding venue just in time for a pre-ceremony photo shoot before guests arrived. Donning a gorgeous flower collar, and with her big brown eyes, she was in true glam form for the wedding photographer. As her adoring parents, we couldn't have been more thrilled to have her there to share in the special moment. It was worth every penny to have her privately escorted, get her glammed up for photos, and spend some quality time with her before the guests arrived.

Lindsey, Lisa & Scout
BOSTON, MASSACHUSETTS

YOU ADOPTED A DOG YOU CAN TRULY RELATE TO BECAUSE YOU FACE SIMILAR CHALLENGES.

When I saw Jellybean's tiny malformed legs, I knew we were destined for one another. I have spinal stenosis, and Jellybean's legs, a birth defect, keep him from being mobile. Sharing this made us immediately closer than we ever could be, and my "soul mutt" and I spoke each other's language right away. Jellybean understands that mornings are hard for me, with pain so unbearable that sometimes I don't even want to get up. But little Jellybean greets me, tail wagging, by smothering me in so many kisses I can hardly breathe! We laugh and play until I can get ready for the adventures of the day, which usually means a bike ride.

Since neither of us can walk around the block, I bought us an adult tricycle with a doggie car seat secured for Jellybean in the basket in back. We bike up to three miles every day! It's great for both of us to experience fresh air and movement. This sweet little soul means everything to me. I owe Jellybean a huge debt of gratitude that I can never repay.

Nancy & Jellybean
AMES, IOWA

YOU ARE YOUR DOG'S PROTECTOR.

I live in a country where many people have a negative opinion of dogs. Some believe that they may make you infertile or that their meat is meant for consumption. People stare at me when I walk my dog, but I can handle the judgment and harsh words. I will always defend my dog, no matter what they throw at us. They simply don't understand the pureness of a dog's heart.

Felicia & Bruno
JAKARTA, INDONESIA 📷 JANE_FELICIAK

YOU SAVED YOUR DOG FROM DEATH ROW AND MADE HIM A FOSTER BROTHER TO HUNDREDS OF ORPHANED RESCUE PUPPIES IN AUSTRALIA (AND IT ONLY TOOK YOU AN ENGAGEMENT RING TO GET THERE).

My husband, Brad, and I saved Pikelet from death row at a local council pound in Sydney, Australia, after years of fostering rescue puppies. With a case of rickets that caused his legs and spine to bend, Pikelet was just five weeks old when his euthanization was scheduled. Luckily, Big Dog Rescue placed him into our foster care. I woke up every day and asked my husband if we could adopt Pikelet, and every day his response was no since we already had two dogs.

Finally, one day he told me that if we found my missing engagement ring that had mysteriously vanished from my bedside table a week prior, then we could adopt Pikelet. We searched for some time, until one cold and rainy morning my husband ran up the stairs to our bedroom and held out a doggie bag filled with Pikey's poop. There, clear as day, was also the smallest glint of silver. Within an hour of finding the ring, Pikelet Butterwiggle Stoll's adoption papers were signed.

In the three years since he was adopted, Pikelet has become Australia's best big foster brother to many orphaned rescue puppies. He takes an instant liking to every single pup that walks into his home and life. Inside his furry Staffy body is a sweet and gentle demeanor that makes him a perfect big brother.

Calley & Pikelet
SYDNEY, AUSTRALIA 🅞 LIFEOFPIKELET

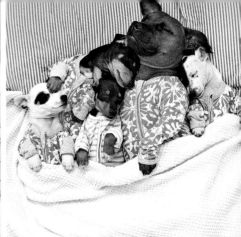

YOU ONLY ACCEPTED YOUR NEW JOB AFTER NEGOTIATING THAT YOUR DOGS COULD COME TOO.

When my then-fiancé, Justin, and I got Brody and Buddy, he worked from home and I was still in college. We promised that we would never leave them alone during the day, no matter what. Justin relocated and started to work in an office from Monday to Friday. I stayed at home just to keep our promise. Now we work together, but I only took the job after convincing our employer to let us bring our boys to work. I can't imagine not seeing their faces and stumpy legs all day long. Plus, the perks of working at a multimedia company mean we get to use our office studio to take photos of them all the time!

Jenay, Brody & Buddy
HAWK POINT, MISSOURI 📷 BROANDBUDCORGIS

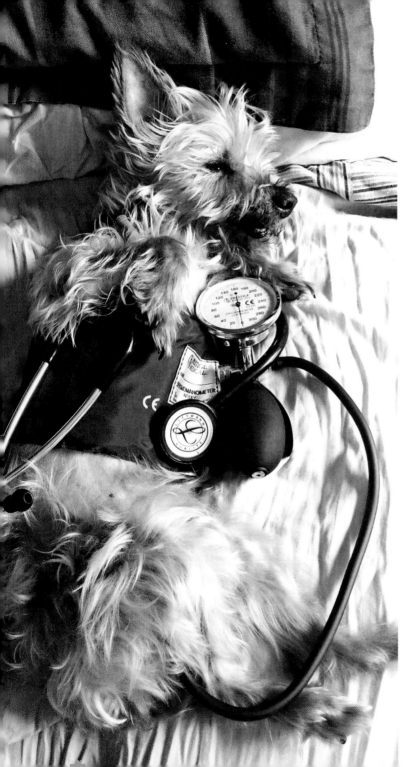

YOU ARE REMINDED TO APPRECIATE EVERY SINGLE DAY WHENEVER YOU SEE YOUR DOG'S CROOKED SMILE.

Since Bonkerz came into my life, he hasn't left my side. Even after he was brutally attacked by another dog, he stayed with me, surviving surgery and months of recovery. Although he was on a liquid diet for a year, Bonk's jaw, which was broken in two places, never fully healed. The result is a crooked, yet charming, smile. He only has four teeth and is blind and deaf. However, none of this dampens his spirit! His love and companionship helped me overcome the darkest days in my life. Bonkerz and his crooked smile are an inspiration to me every single day.

Mariah & Bonkerz
WESLEY CHAPEL, FLORIDA

YOU ADOPTED A DOG TO
FIND A COMPANION
AND ENDED UP FINDING
A RAISON D'ÊTRE.

For me, adopting a senior dog was a lifestyle choice. I'm not that active and feared I couldn't give a younger dog all the exercise it needed. While I love dogs of all ages, I prefer older ones in my home. They are less likely to chew on my shoes and don't require constant supervision. When I adopted Chloe, I didn't realize how many senior dogs live in shelters. They end up there for a variety of reasons: because they got old and undesirable, because their owners are unable to care for them (like Chloe's was), or sadly because their owner passed away. I originally rescued a senior dog for practical reasons, but it has evolved into an important mission. I'm honored to be a part of a growing movement committed to rescuing senior dogs.

Dorie & Chloe Kardoggian
NEW YORK, NEW YORK 📷 CHLOEKARDOGGIAN

RAISON D'ÊTRE (razôn detre) n.
The most important reason or purpose for someone or something's existence. See also: dinner

YOU ADOPTED A DOG WITH A FEW WEEKS TO LIVE AND GAVE HER THE BEST WEEKS POSSIBLE.

Fourteen-year-old Clover, who had mammary tumors, was found by a farmer, abandoned at the side of the road. The farmer posted to her Facebook page that Clover was causing trouble (read: eating chickens) and would be euthanized if she was not claimed. An hour after seeing the posting, I picked her up. I didn't care that heartbreak would likely come soon; I immediately knew that I had to bring her home.

Clover was a spitfire from day one. She knocked over the trash can, chased our chickens, escaped from the deck three times, and found a bag of food. One thing was patently clear: Clover still had life to live. To make the most of the time Clover had left, I created a bucket list. The list had vet visits (not her favorite), shopping sprees, bath time, road trips, family pictures, pawdicures, go-to-work-with-Mom days, cheeseburgers and steak meals, fruit stand visits, and sleepovers.

In the seven short weeks I had with Clover, I fell head over heels in love. She taught me about forgiveness, trust, and resilience. As I held her for the last time, I knew, without a doubt, that she went peacefully, knowing what it is to be loved.

Amanda & Clover
BENT MOUNTAIN, VIRGINIA

YOU LEAVE YOUR DOG WITH THREE PET BEDS EVERY TIME YOU ARE OUT OF THE HOUSE.

I am absolutely and utterly in love with my baby Brussels Griffon, Penny (Penelope) Pruna. I thought I was getting a puppy when I adopted her, but I ended up with the most loving cat/dog/bird/deer a person could ask for.

I once bought a cat house for my sister's new kitten and we came home that night to find Penny perched on top of it. She didn't move from it, just looked up at us as if to say "What's so funny?" Since she's one-quarter cat, I make sure to leave her three different pet beds by the balcony doors and windows so she can easily watch the ducks in the lake while I'm at work all day.

Jocelyn, Art & Penny
MIAMI, FLORIDA 📷 PENNYGRIFFON

YOU WROTE A BOOK AND MADE A LIVING OUT OF DOODLING DOGS.

I grew up with dogs from a young age, so dogs have always been part of my life. I love mixed mutts. My first dog was a feral stray named Shag. If that dog had been a person, he would have been out on the corner smoking a cigar. It was just one of those wild dogs—the kind that's impossible to housetrain. We actually caught Shag mating with the neighbor's dog. It was like a movie. You're a kid and you walk in the front yard and they're just going at it.

Dogs to me, above all animals, are the most personality-oriented. I also think that all people project their own feelings onto dogs, so that's a fun aspect to doodling them. Dogs really want to

THIS GUY DREW ALL THE DOODLES IN THIS BOOK!

THIS DOG DID THIS DRAWING OF THE ILLUSTRATOR

MACY YOU AR
tHE BEST DOG EVR
HERE AR
tREATS
FOR YOU!!!

know what you want them to do. They really pay attention to how people are behaving. I think the fact that they have personalities really lends itself to cartoons like that.

My dog, Macy, is a little rescue dog mix. If I could talk to her, I think I would ask her just what she thinks about when she's just lying around. I often wonder what dogs dream about. I also want to know what they are thinking more than anything.

And, I'd also ask for cartoon ideas.

Dave & Macy
DETROIT, MICHIGAN | SPEEDBUMP.COM

"If I'm being honest with myself, they're not really 'accidents'."